HORACE GREELEY AND THE POLITICS OF REFORM IN NINETEENTH-CENTURY AMERICA

AMERICAN PROFILES

Norman K. Risjord, Series Editor

Thomas Jefferson
  By Norman K. Risjord
Mary Boykin Chesnut: A Confederate Woman's Life
  By Mary A. DeCredico
John Quincy Adams
  By Lynn Hudson Parsons
He Shall Go Out Free: The Lives of Denmark Vesey
  By Douglas R. Egerton
Samuel Adams: America's Revolutionary Politician
  By John K. Alexander
Jefferson's America, 1760–1815: Second Edition
  By Norman K. Risjord
Martin Van Buren and the Emergence of American Popular Politics
  By Joel H. Silbey
*He Shall Go Out Free: The Lives of Denmark Vesey, Revised and
  Updated Edition*
  By Douglas R. Egerton
Stephan A. Douglas and the Dilemmas of Democratic Equality
  By James L. Huston
William Jennings Bryan: An Uncertain Trumpet
  By Gerald Leinwand
*Horace Greeley and the Politics of Reform in Nineteenth-Century
  America*
  By Mitchell Snay

HORACE GREELEY AND THE POLITICS OF REFORM IN NINETEENTH-CENTURY AMERICA

Mitchell Snay

ROWMAN & LITTLEFIELD PUBLISHERS, INC.
Lanham • Boulder • New York • Toronto • Plymouth, UK

Published by Rowman & Littlefield Publishers, Inc.
A wholly owned subsidiary of The Rowman & Littlefield Publishing Group, Inc.
4501 Forbes Boulevard, Suite 200, Lanham, Maryland 20706
http://www.rowmanlittlefield.com

Estover Road, Plymouth PL6 7PY, United Kingdom

British Library Cataloguing in Publication Information Available

Library of Congress Cataloging-in-Publication Data

Snay, Mitchell.
  Horace Greeley and the politics of reform in nineteenth-century America /
Mitchell Snay.
      p. cm. — (American profiles)
  Includes bibliographical references and index.
  ISBN 978-0-7425-5100-8 (cloth : alk. paper) — ISBN 978-1-4422-1002-8
(electronic)
  1. Greeley, Horace, 1811–1872. 2. Presidential candidates—United States—
Biography. 3. Newspaper editors—New York (State)—New York—Biography.
4. Politicians—United States—Biography. 5. United States—Politics and
government—1849–1877. I. Title.
  E415.9.G8S63 2011
  070.92—dc22
  [B]   2011010376

Printed in the United States of America

For my teachers:

Dawn McKee Wyman at Mather High School
James O. Horton at the University of Michigan
Marvin Meyers at Brandeis University

Contents

Acknowledgments   ix

Introduction   1

1. From Country to City:
Coming of Age in the Early Republic   7

2. The Politics of Whiggery: The 1830s   21

3. The World of Print Culture in
Antebellum New York   49

4. The Politics of Reform: The 1840s   65

5. The Politics of Antislavery: The 1850s   93

6. The Politics of Union: The Civil War   131

7. The Politics of Reconstruction   155

Bibliography   183

Index   189

About the Author   199

Acknowledgments

THE RELATIVE SPEED with which I was able to research and write this book surprised me. For this, I owe thanks to a number of individuals and institutions who supported and advanced this endeavor.

A year's sabbatical from Denison University allowed me the time for research and provided the resources for visiting archives. Librarians and staff at the Ohio Historical Society, the New York Public Library, the New York Historical Society, the Manuscripts Division of the Library of Congress, and the University of Rochester helped make Horace Greeley's manuscripts accessible. The librarians at Denison were especially generous in lending out microfilm reels of the *New York Tribune*.

Sean Wilentz, Michael F. Holt, Iver Bernstein, and Jonathan H. Earle gave encouraging and helpful comments on an early book proposal. Subsequently, Michael Holt gave a careful reading of a completed manuscript that saved me from numerous factual errors. Diane Sommerville also read a draft and gave helpful stylistic suggestions. At Rowman & Littlefield, Laura Roberts Gottleib, Michael McGandy, Neils Aboe, Patricia Stevenson, and above all Sarah David contributed in moving the project toward publication. I owe a special thanks to Norman Risjord, the editor of the American Profile Series. His interest in the project remained steadfast over the years, and he read with great care several drafts of the manuscript.

My trips to New York were made much easier and much more enjoyable by the hospitality of Stan and Charlotte Plotnick, my Uncle Stan and Aunt Charlotte. I still treasure our trips to the Second Avenue Deli and Yankee Stadium. My sister Abby and brother-in-law Ed remain faithful and loving supporters of my professional endeavors. Closest to home, my wife Liz and son Elliott inadvertently carved out more time for me to write as they were meeting the heavy demands of their own lives. As my family, they remain the anchor and boon of my life.

The dedication pays tribute to three very special history teachers. In their own distinctive ways, they changed my life by showing me my calling and keeping me on my professional journey. In many ways, my entire career in history—both teaching and writing—has been an extended effort to honor them.

Introduction

HORACE GREELEY WAS BORN in the small New England town of Amherst, New Hampshire, in 1811. He began working as a newspaper apprentice in Vermont. In 1831, Greeley arrived in New York, where he would spend the rest of his editorial career. The *New-Yorker*, Greeley's first venture into independent journalism, began publication in the spring of 1834 when he was twenty-three years old. He then edited two Whig partisan sheets, the *Jeffersonian* and the *Log Cabin*. In 1841, Greeley founded the *New York Tribune*, which would become the one of the nation's leading newspapers. He was also a leader in the state and national Whig Party and would be a major figure in the formation of the Republican Party during the 1850s. In 1872, he ran unsuccessfully for president on the Liberal Republican ticket. He died later that year. Greeley was also well known as a reformer whose causes included antislavery, temperance, Fourierism, and land reform.

The life of Horace Greeley corresponds closely to what used to be known as the "Middle Period" of American history. This era traditionally begins in 1815 with the end of the War of 1812, when Greeley was four years old, and terminates in 1877 when the removal of federal troops from the South ended Reconstruction, five years after his death. The decades in between witnessed profound changes in the American economic, social, and political order. As a newspaper editor, reformer, and politician, Greeley reflected these changes and

helped shape a response to them. This book explores the public life
of Horace Greeley in its historical context in order to better understand the transformations of the nineteenth-century United States.

During Greeley's lifetime, the United States metamorphosed
from an agrarian republic into an industrial nation-state. The early
nineteenth century witnessed a process of economic development

Portrait of Horace Greeley, dated 1872. (Courtesy of the Library of Congress)

and modernization. Revolutions in transportation and communication catalyzed and accompanied the advent of capitalism. The telegraph and the proliferation of books, magazines, and newspapers dramatically increased the flow and diffusion of information. Politically, the expansion of democracy through increased suffrage led to the institutionalization of American politics in a two-party system. These material changes, along with the continued influx of European patterns of thought, transformed the American cultural landscape into one dominated by individualism, evangelical religion, and a search for a national identity. The simultaneous development of these forces gave birth to a distinctive middle class. This new class, closely tied to first the Whig then the Republican Party, would constitute the main audience of Greeley's *Tribune*.

Two themes dominate the narrative of U.S. history between the War of 1812 and Reconstruction. One is the sectional conflict over slavery. The invention of the cotton gin fastened a regime of staple-crop agriculture and plantation slavery on the South that expanded southwesterly during the period. Abolitionist agitation from the North beginning in the early 1830s awakened a nascent defense of slavery as a positive good. This ideological controversy over slavery entered the political party system when the acquisition of new land after the Mexican-American War raised the question of slavery in the territories. Sectional antagonisms over the expansion of slavery fractured the party system during the 1850s. The ensuing secession of eleven Southern states and the defeat of the Confederacy in the Civil War doomed chattel slavery in the United States.

The rise of industrial capitalism is the other dominant theme. The capitalist transformation of America changed the nature of work, as independent artisans gradually gave way to dependent wage earners. A growing working class, with separate neighborhoods and distinctive leisure activities, had emerged in urban America by the 1830s. For the next four decades, workers sought to protect and advance their interests through strikes, labor unions, and independent political action. The Civil War greatly accelerated both industrialization and class conflict, exemplified in the New York City draft riots of 1863. By the 1870s, the "labor question" was arguably the most pressing issue in America both North and South.

Sectional and labor conflicts thus provide the two underlying themes in this biography of Horace Greeley. They clarify his role as a political spokesman for the Whig and Republican parties and help explain why he was at the center of every major reform movement of the era. Greeley illustrates one pattern of nineteenth-century politics by showing how moral issues like temperance or slavery became political and partisan questions.

The richness of change in the Jacksonian era has led one historian to characterize these years as an "Age of Ambiguity." American life was pulled in contradictory directions—between majority rule and minority rights, liberty and order, individualism and community, and optimism and fear. Greeley embodied several of these tensions. For instance, he remained an advocate of individualized capitalism in cooperative structures. He actively supported the formation of labor unions, though he never strayed from his ideal of class harmony. He sought the elevation of the working class while resisting the formation of class and class consciousness. He fought for the abolition of slavery, but remained ambivalent about the role of the state in securing equality and civil rights for African Americans. In essence, the life and thought of Horace Greeley reveal the deepest American contradictions over race, class, and democracy.

Greeley's attempt to navigate the ambivalent age of Andrew Jackson and Abraham Lincoln became evident in a set of ideas that provided some unity to his public life. Although these ideas are difficult to label with any ideological precision, Greeley and his contemporaries often characterized their efforts at "liberal" reform. Clearly, these ideas do not conform to the classical European liberalism of figures like John Stuart Mill who clung tenaciously to laissez-faire economics and free trade. In the United States, this kind of free-trade liberalism, embodied in the Liberal Republican revolt of 1872, marked a conscious retreat from government intervention. Despite his nomination in 1872 by the Liberal Republicans, Greeley remained a committed supporter of the protective tariff.

What Greeley meant by "liberal" is perhaps closer to what historian Sean Wilentz has recently characterized as "new school Whiggery." As much as anyone else, Greeley embodied the values and programs of younger, more progressive Whigs who supported a national bank, a protective tariff, and the distribution of public lands. Greeley and other like-minded Whigs endorsed democratic movements of national independence in Europe. His support for government-supported programs of economic growth and moral improvement transferred into the Republican Party of the 1850s and 1860s.

Along with its value in illustrating his era, the life of Horace Greeley is fascinating in its own right. At the *Tribune*, Greeley gathered around him an array of young intellectuals that included George William Curtis, Margaret Fuller, Mark Twain, and Karl Marx. He was friends with circus promoter P. T. Barnum and Transcendentalist recluse Henry David Thoreau. He corresponded regularly with presidents, senators, and other public figures. Usually seen in his white hat and long white coat, he struck his contemporaries as a bit peculiar. Greeley could be difficult and contentious in dealings with people. Henry Clapp once described him as a "self-made man who worshipped his creator." Greeley's marriage and family life were filled with conflict and tragedy. Personal happiness forever eluded him.

Despite brief excursions into the private sphere, this book concentrates on Greeley's career as an editor, reformer, and politician. It uses this life as a means to illuminate the central themes and tensions of the period between the War of 1812 and the end of Reconstruction. It is thus not only a story of one very significant historical figure but also a history of an era that gave birth to modern America.

Chapter One

―――――――――――――○―――――――――――――

From Country to City
Coming of Age in the Early Republic

IN 1868, HORACE GREELEY PUBLISHED his autobiography under the title *Recollections of a Busy Life*. By dedicating the volume "To Our American Boys, who, born in poverty, cradled in obscurity, and early called from school to rugged labor, are seeking to convert obstacle into opportunity, and wrest achievement from difficulty," Greeley paid homage both to himself and to the nineteenth-century myth of free labor mobility. For the writing of his *Recollections* involved not only creating a narrative of his childhood but also constructing an image of an idyllic rural republic in early nineteenth-century New England. Greeley's efforts reflected an American penchant to look back and idealize a pastoral past of stability, virtue, and innocence that contrasted with the unrestrained mobility and disorder of contemporary society.

His childhood world was, according to Greeley, a rural Garden of Eden: "There was more humor, more play, more fun, more merriment, in that Puritan community, than can be found anywhere in this anxious, plodding age." Unlike the visible extremes of wealth evident in the mid-nineteenth century, Greeley's family and neighbors all were "measurably poor, yet seldom were any hungry." He glorified their sense of community. "House-raisings, corn-huskings, and all manner of excuses for festive merry-making," Greeley recalled, "were frequent, and generally improved." Humanity prospered in such an idyllic world. "Happily, living in frugal plenty, almost wholly on their own products, spending much of their time in vigorous exercise in the open air, and having but one doctor within call," Greeley insisted, "they had great tenacity of life."

Born in New Hampshire in 1811, Horace Greeley grew up in the Granite State and in nearby Vermont. Educated in the common schools of New England, he received his first apprenticeship as a printer in Poultney, Vermont. In 1831, his ambition took him to New York City. The journey from country to city was common to many aspiring American men who became prominent in the era of the Civil War. P. T. Barnum, for example, was born in Bethel, Connecticut, and radical Republican Thaddeus Stevens hailed from Danville, Vermont. The Massachusetts countryside produced educational reformer Horace Mann and merchants and antislavery campaigners Arthur and Lewis Tappan. Greeley acquired a set of values that he maintained throughout his life in the New England village. It was here that he learned to attach a moral significance to labor that would serve as a compass during his career, shaping his approach to industrialization and the sectional controversy over slavery.

I

Horace Greeley's ancestors were firmly rooted in the soil of Puritan New England. In 1640, three Greeley brothers migrated to America. One Andrew Greeley settled in Salisbury, Massachusetts. His descendents eventually migrated into New Hampshire, where Horace's grandfather Zaccheus was born in 1752. Zaccheus, a yeoman farmer who reputedly knew the Bible by heart, served as the model yeoman farmer for Greeley: "I think few men were more sincerely and generally esteemed than he by those who knew him." Greeley's father, also called Zaccheus, was born in 1782. In 1807, he married Mary Woodburn, who also—in the words of one Greeley biographer—came from an "undistinguished, middle-class, small-town, and country folk, mostly farmers and blacksmiths." From contemporary accounts, Horace's mother Mary emerges as a strong and gregarious spirit. Absorbing the folklore of her Scotch-Irish ancestors, she spent much of her time in the fields singing.

She danced and smoked a pipe as well. Young Horace would often fill the pipe with tobacco and light it for her.

Zaccheus and Mary Greeley bought a farm about five miles from Amherst, New Hampshire, where Horace Greeley was born on February 3, 1811. His birth was precarious—he could not breathe for the first twenty minutes of his life. According to Greeley biographer Robert C. Williams, one possible result of early oxygen deprivation is Asperger's Syndrome, a mild form of autism that might help account for Horace's often difficult social relationships later in life. Altogether, Zaccheus and Mary had five children: two sons and three daughters.

Two aspects of Greeley's childhood—labor and education—would be of particular and lasting significance. It was on the family farm that Greeley "first learned that this is a world of hard work." As a farmer's son, Greeley "was early made acquainted with labor." He planted corn, cut wood, and picked out stones from "those rocky New England farms." From Mary Greeley, Horace inherited his love of reading and learning. He recalled his mother as "a most omnivorous and retentive reader" who had learned from her Irish mother an "abundant store of ballads, stories, anecdotes, and traditions." Horace was reading by the time he was three years old. He first started school at four, an age at which he claimed being "specially clever in spelling." The first book Greeley ever owned was *The Columbian Orator*, his "prized text-book for years." (This book also proved to be the turning point for another reformer and foe of slavery, the former slave Frederick Douglass.) Young Greeley was considered so precocious that the townspeople offered to pay for him to attend Exeter Academy, but his family refused what they saw as an offer of charity. Consequently, the future editor of the *New York Tribune* ended his formal schooling when he was thirteen.

The Panic of 1819, which occurred when Greeley was eight years old, was the first major economic crisis to hit the young American republic. He recalled that "almost every one owed, and scarcely any one could pay." Horace awoke on a Monday in August to find the family farm foreclosed. The family managed to pay off some of their creditors, but they were "as bankrupt a family as well could be." In January 1821, the Greeley family moved to Westhaven, Vermont,

where they "took rank with day-laborers." His father chopped wood
for fifty cents a day. Greeley himself was a farm laborer until he was
fifteen years old.

His autobiography reveals ambivalence about his agrarian past.
Although he engaged in youthful outdoor activities, he was not well
suited physically for hard agricultural labor. "In the farmer's calling,
as I saw it followed," Greeley remembered further, "there was neither scope for expanding faculties, incitement to constant growth
in knowledge, nor a spur to generous ambition." On the other hand,
Greeley admired the state of republican simplicity in early New
England. He recalled that his family "never needed nor ran into
debt for anything; never were without meal, meat, and wood, and
very rarely without money." Since his family lost its farm, these recollections almost certainly masked painful memories of uncertainty
and poverty in hard economic times.

Journalism—rather than farming—became Horace Greeley's
true calling. At eleven years of age, his father took him to a local
printer for work. Though Greeley was fascinated by the work, the
printer was not interested in such a young helper. In 1826, when he
was fifteen, he walked to East Poultney, Vermont, to ask for a job
at the *Northern Spectator*, a Federalist newspaper edited by Amos
Bliss and E. G. Stone. He agreed to an apprenticeship on April 18,
1826 (a date obviously important enough for him to remember),
while his father moved west in search of a better farm. Horace
agreed to work for five years. For the first six months, he would
receive only room and board. After that, the apprentice would get
forty dollars a year.

"He was then a remarkably plain-looking unsophisticated lad of
fifteen," a fellow worker recalled, "with a slouching, careless gait,
leaning away forward as he walked, as if both his head and his heels
were too heavy for his body." Greeley's apprenticeship proved difficult: "Few apprentices worked more steadily and faithfully than I
did throughout the four years and over half my stay in Poultney."
He learned to set type, work the Ramage press, and condense news
from other newspapers. Greeley absorbed information quickly and
soon became known for his vast arsenal of political knowledge. He
later claimed that his apprenticeship at a newspaper was a better
education than four years in college.

In 1830, Horace left the *Spectator* and Poultney, Vermont. He first visited his father in the town of Clymer in western Pennsylvania. Greeley recalled the hardships of travel before railroads: "He who will measure his walk by mile-stones, as I have done, will discover that lively and persistent stepping, with no stopping to chase butterflies, is required to make four miles per hour." While in Clymer, Greeley worked on his father's farm chopping wood. It was not to his liking, though: "Fully convinced that the life of a pioneer was one to which I was poorly adapted, I made one more effort to resume my chosen calling." He worked briefly for the Erie *Gazette*, where journeymen and apprenticed printers boarded at the house of the owner, Joseph M. Sterret. Greeley's next job in journalism would take him away from rural New England and into New York City.

II

To understand how these early years in rural New England influenced Greeley's public career, it is necessary to sketch out some of the social and economic changes reshaping the region at this time. The northeastern United States was quickly becoming a capitalist and democratic society. In 1815, the *Niles' Weekly Register* noted "the almost universal ambition to get forward" in America. By the 1830s, the French observer Alexis de Tocqueville coined a term to capture the essence of this new democratic society: *individualism*. It was this social and political order that would be celebrated by the editor and reformer Greeley.

The "Market Revolution" lay at the foundation of this transformation of rural New England. During the late eighteenth century, most farmers aimed at what was called a "competence"—economic self-sufficiency with the ability to protect the long-term independence of the household. It was a rural economy based on the family labor of the husband, wife, and children. The materials they could not produce themselves could be purchased in local markets or bartered for the goods they raised beyond subsistence.

Demographic growth over the course of the eighteenth century forced changes in this system. The rural population of New England continued to grow from natural increase, and the expanding population put pressure on existing supplies of land, reducing the size of the landholdings of average rural families. One response to this situation was mobility. Many New Englanders migrated to the unsettled areas of Vermont, New Hampshire, and Maine. Zaccheus Greeley, for example, moved west to seek new lands. Another response was to look for new ways to gain income from the soil, such as experimenting with new crops. Many New England farmers in the early nineteenth century ventured into dairying, for example.

A third response—in the opinion of most historians, the one with the most long-term consequences—was to engage more fully in an expanding market economy. Rural markets had existed in the eighteenth century, but they broadened considerably with the expansion of roads, canals, steamboats, and eventually railroads. By reducing the time and cost of transportation, these "internal improvements" expanded access to markets. In addition, the Napoleonic Wars of the 1790s and 1800s increased the European market for American foodstuffs. Within the household, production of nonfarm goods rose as a way to gain more income. With the help of rural entrepreneurs who furnished the raw materials, farm families produced finished goods like brooms, shoes, hides, cloth, and even furniture; in his *Recollections*, Greeley recalled that the production of cloth "was effected by the simplest manual labor." With the additional income came improved standards of living. Rural New England homes were now furnished with chairs, clocks, and individual place settings with knives, forks, and china plates.

Greeley's mother spun wool and linen for nearby cotton mills, but she eventually lost her job because of cheaper British cloth imports. The Greeley family's experiences with rural manufacturing made Horace an early advocate of protective tariffs. He would cling to this principle throughout his life, even in the 1872 Liberal Republican campaign. Greeley blamed the distress of 1819 on the plethora of British goods dumped on American markets. "I have not been much of a Free-Trader ever since," he recalled. Because the wool industry was important in Vermont, many in the state supported John Quincy Adams for president in 1828 due to his advocacy of protection.

III

The modernization of the New England economy was accompanied by the democratization of politics. The American Revolution had unleashed an ideology of republicanism that stressed equality and independence. Simultaneously, it ushered in a series of social changes that eroded the traditional deference to established elites and brought new, previously marginalized groups into the political process. Yet the rise of democracy in the early republic remained a matter of dispute. Many Americans questioned the egalitarian direction of change and sought to curb democracy through political and constitutional means. The clash over the extent of democratization became institutionalized in the first American political parties, established in the 1790s: the Jeffersonian Republicans and the Federalists. Followers of Thomas Jefferson maintained a faith in the wisdom of the people, while the more commercialized Federalists argued that social order required limitations on the rule of the people.

By the early nineteenth century, rural New England was disproportionately Federalist. In Amherst and Bedford, New Hampshire—where Horace Greeley came of age—most voters were ardent Federalists. In the election of 1800, Jefferson garnered only two votes from nearby Londonderry. Both of Horace's parents were Federalists who read the *Farmer's Cabinet*, the party newspaper from Amherst. Yet in his *Recollections*, Greeley played down his Federalist roots. Rather, he claimed that his family and neighbors in rural New Hampshire were, "in the truest sense, democrats." The family servants even ate with the family. "Nowhere were manners ever simpler, or society freer from pretension or exclusiveness," Greeley maintained, "than in those farmers' homes."

The crusade of anti-Masonry in the late 1820s and early 1830s was a striking illustration of the democratization of politics. In 1826, a former Mason in western New York, William Morgan, published an exposé critical of the fraternal order of Freemasonry. Morgan was arrested on a most likely fabricated charge and put into the jail in Canandaigua. He was then released from jail, but disappeared soon after. By most accounts, Morgan had been abducted and murdered by Masons incensed that he had divulged secrets of the order. Morgan's disappearance unleashed a wave of hostility to secret aristocratic societies, which spread like wildfire throughout New York and New England. It begat an egalitarian social movement and political party that drew in thousands of disgruntled voters. In the presidential election of 1832, the Anti-Masonic Party nominated William Wirt for president.

Despite the alacrity and notoriety of the phenomenon, anti-Masonry soon expired. Wirt garnered less than 10 percent of the popular vote. Nevertheless, anti-Masonry would leave an indelible impression on Jacksonian politics. "Anti-Masonry had divided us," Greeley later recalled, "and driven thousands of Adams men over to Jackson, whose personal popularity was very great, especially with the non-reading class, and who had strengthened himself at the North by his Tariff Messages and his open rupture with Calhoun."

IV

Democratization was also manifested in religion. The Revolution had unleashed religion from its moorings in officially sanctioned state churches. Although the Congregational Church retained its state status in some areas of New England until 1833, the Revolution had dissolved the formal union of church and state everywhere else. State-sponsored churches were replaced by competing denominations that, like political parties, vied for the allegiance of the people. The Methodists and Baptists spread rapidly in the Revolutionary era. The latter had no adherents in 1760, but by 1790 had more than seven hundred churches. By 1820, the Baptist Church had over 250,000 formal members. The early republic also witnessed the Second Great Awakening (the first had occurred in the 1740s and 1750s), which, according to historian Gordon S. Wood, "marked the beginning of the republicanizing and nationalizing of American religion." Thus, religiosity in rural New England remained vibrant and vital.

New Hampshire had become a refuge for religious dissenters like Baptists, Methodists, and Presbyterians. Greeley soon became attached to another denomination spawned by the religious ferment of the early republic, the Universalists. As the name suggested, this new denomination promised salvation to any seekers. Rejecting the Calvinist principle of original sin and damnation, they stressed that the evangelical, immediate experience of the Divine was open to everyone. The Universalists organized twenty-three churches in the Connecticut River valley of Vermont between 1795 and 1815. Directed by religious leaders like Hosea Ballou, the Universalists had a special appeal to the rural intelligentsia of New England. Justin Morrill, later to achieve fame as a Republican legislator, was another Vermont editor to embrace Universalism.

Setting a pattern for the next few decades of the nineteenth century, the beliefs of the Second Great Awakening spawned many of the reforms and "-isms" that would characterize antebellum America. Temperance—the avoidance and repudiation of alcohol—was perhaps the most popular one. Early reformers such as Benjamin Rush urged temperance as part of a larger effort to create a virtuous citizenry necessary for the survival of a republic. Initially temperance leaders were closely linked to the Federalist Party. Temperance was viewed as an antidote to what Federalists saw as an excess of individualism and democracy. The Panic of 1819 abetted the movement, as reformers linked intemperance and pauperism. In 1825, Dr. Justin Edwards published *The Well-Conducted Farm*, which drew a connection between sobriety and economic stability, a message that Greeley would have endorsed. Greeley believed his father's financial problems were related to drinking. In 1824, he became a convert to temperance and helped form a local temperance society the next year. In 1826, this reform movement was institutionalized in the formation of the American Society for the Promotion of Temperance.

Similar to other prominent nineteenth-century figures, Greeley's upbringing in rural New England set patterns of beliefs and models of social relations that would significantly inform his career in journalism, reform, and politics. Coming of age in the early republic gave Greeley a faith in progress, or what the nineteenth century knew as "improvement." Throughout his life, he retained a belief in the individual and social benefits of free enterprise, aided occasionally and selectively by government intervention. An idealized vision of the harmony of rural social relations would persist into the period of class formation and increasingly bitter class conflict in the 1860s and 1870s. Greeley's immersion in the faith of Revolutionary republicanism gave him a lifelong attachment to freedom that would become the basis for his opposition to slavery. When Horace Greeley left for New York City in 1831, the moral atmosphere of the country had thus left indelible and lasting impressions on him.

V

Greeley arrived in New York on August 17, 1831. "I was twenty years old the preceding February," he recalled, "tall, slender, pale, and plain, with ten dollars in my pocket, Summer clothing worth perhaps as much more, nearly all on my back, and a decent knowledge of so much of the art of printing as a boy will usually learn in the office of a country newspaper." Following his literary and editorial apprenticeship in Vermont, Greeley began looking for work with newspapers. Since New York contained thousands of young printers seeking similar employment, his first efforts were discouraging: "I returned to my lodging on Saturday evening, thoroughly weary, disheartened, disgusted with New York, and resolved to shake its dust from my feet next Monday morning, while I could still leave with money in my pocket, and before its almshouse could foreclose upon me." Persistence, however, paid off. His first printing job came with John T. West at 85 Chatham Street, composing a pocketbook edition of the New Testament. During the following winter, Greeley took jobs with a variety of newspapers: the *Evening Post*, the *Commercial Advertiser*, and a sporting journal, the *Spirit of the Times*.

Greeley entered a new urban world in 1831. No less than its rural counterpart, urban America had experienced significant transformation between 1790 and 1830. In 1790, the population of New York had stood at 33,131. The next two decades witnessed a rise in

Map of New York City in the mid-nineteenth century, created by John Bachman. (Courtesy of the Library of Congress)

shipping due to increased demand for American foodstuffs during the Napoleonic Wars, and thanks to its port, New York became the nation's largest city. Its population in 1810 was already at 96,373. Furthermore, the completion of the Erie Canal in 1825 made New York City the emporium of the nation. It captured a major share of the nation's import business from 1821 to 1836. Commerce transformed the economic and social landscape of New York. New wharves appeared along the Hudson and East Rivers. New institutions to support trade, such as insurance and banking, appeared. Wall Street, with the Merchant's Exchange, became the financial center of New York. By 1840, there were 417 commercial houses dedicated to foreign trade and 918 commission firms that dealt with domestic markets. The rise in trade spurred new industries like shipbuilding, printing, and the production of leather, furniture, and shoes. The pace of commercial life that heightened the demand for residential space paved the way for new hotels in the 1820s and 1830s.

A new bourgeoisie was taking shape in early nineteenth-century New York. The increase in trade allowed for the amassing of large individual fortunes. While per-capita wealth in New York rose 60 percent between 1790 and 1826, the wealthiest 4 percent of the city's population owned more than half the wealth. This growing prosperity provided the foundation for a consumer economy and society. New dry goods stores catered to an affluent middle class. In 1818, Connecticut merchant Henry Sands Brooks founded a men's clothing store that his sons would rename Brooks Brothers. In 1826, Samuel Lord and George Washington Taylor began to sell "elegant Cashmere shawls" for women. The mercantile elite shared social and cultural as well as economic bonds. Its members formed exclusive social clubs like the Kent Club, the St. Nicholas Society, the Hone Club, and the Union Club. They helped create an Athenaeum in 1824 that sponsored lectures. Urban gentry supported artists like Thomas Cole and Samuel F. B. Morse and writers like William Cullen Bryant and James Fenimore Cooper.

The economic transformation of early nineteenth-century New York also gave rise to an urban working class. Metropolitan industrialization changed the nature of work, as labor gradually shifted from independent artisans to wage earners. Journeymen were replaced by cheaper labor performed by semi-skilled laborers. The urban geography of New York reflected the rise of a laboring class. The number of people living in the five boroughs reached 242,278 by 1830. Over a fifth were foreign born, and 13,976 were African Americans. The emerging proletariat converged around areas like New York's Five Points, which the New York *Evening Post* claimed was "inhabited by a race of beings of all colours, ages, sexes, and nations." Working-class neighborhoods supported a distinctive leisure culture based around taverns, gambling dens, and theaters. There was a dramatic rise of prostitution in New York during the 1820s. One estimate posits that 5 to 10 percent of women between the ages of fifteen and thirty entered the sex trade. Since prostitutes were especially prominent at Corlear's Hook near the shipyards and ironworks, these women (according to at least one legend) became known as "Hookers."

VI

Horace Greeley spent the next forty years of his life working in New York, closely identifying with the promise and problems of the city. Yet he never forgot the values he inherited from growing up in the New England countryside during the early republic. His career as an editor, reformer, and politician was shaped by both his rural background and his encounter with America's largest city. This combination would continually allow Greeley to create a message that would resonate with a wide range of Americans of his generation. During the 1830s, it determined and informed his strong commitment to the politics of the Whig Party. Yet it would raise tensions between liberty and order and individualism and community. The presidency of Andrew Jackson created opportunities for Americans to express their sentiments on the effects of rapid social, economic, and cultural change that defined the United States in the early nineteenth century.

Chapter Two

───────○───────

The Politics
of Whiggery

The 1830s

THE ELECTION OF 1840 REPRESENTED the high point of Jacksonian democracy. The campaign of "Tippecanoe and Tyler Too" pitted sitting but unpopular Democratic president Martin Van Buren against Whig William Henry Harrison, military hero of the War of 1812. The Whigs adopted the style of popular politics of Jacksonian Democrats and turned it effectively against them. In an attempt to demean the Whig candidate, one Democratic journalist claimed that if given a log cabin and a barrel of hard cider, Harrison would no longer aspire to the presidency. The Democratic editor had inadvertently handed the Whigs a campaign theme. With great fanfare and frenzy, Harrison became the "Log-Cabin and Hard-Cider Candidate." Throughout the country, Whig clubs raised log cabins. Whig supporters danced to the "Tippecanoe Quick Step" and bought Tippecanoe Shaving Soap and Harrison and Tyler neckties. In an era when liquor and politics made familiar bedfellows, Whig supporters could drink Old Cabin Whiskey from bottles shaped like log cabins (its manufacturer, the E. C. Booz Company of Philadelphia, thus added a new word to American English).

The nineteenth-century writer James Parton remembered the "delirium of those mad months." Horace Greeley recollected that "every hour the excitement and enthusiasm swelled higher and higher." Colorful campaigners abounded. John W. Bear of Ohio, the "Buckeye Blacksmith," made 331 speeches in eight states. The thirty-one-year-old Whig Abraham Lincoln stumped the Illinois prairies for Harrison. "Our opponents struggled manfully, desperately," Greeley recalled, "but wind and tide were against them." The Whigs rode their log cabin campaign to great success in the fall of 1840. In a close popular vote but electoral landslide, Harrison defeated Van Buren to become the first Whig president.

The presidential election of 1840 climaxed the partisan strife of the 1830s. In what historians have termed the "Second American Party System," Whigs and Democrats battled over the substance and symbols of economic modernization and political democratization. Greeley's public life during the 1830s revolved around the politics of Jacksonian democracy. "An eager, omnivorous reader, especially of newspapers from early childhood," Greeley wrote in his autobiography, "I was an ardent politician when not yet half old enough to vote." In 1831, while working in Erie, Pennsylvania, Greeley recalled "an intense addiction to partisan strife." Politics seemed to the young man "the universal and engrossing topic."

The contest between Whigs and Democrats gave shape and direction to Greeley's career. His editorial talents attracted the attention of New York Whig leaders Thurlow Weed and William Henry Seward, who took him under their wings. For the next two decades, Greeley, Weed, and Seward became a potent political triumvirate in both state and national politics.

As an editor of several political and literary journals during this period, Greeley began to formulate a political ideology that would shape the rest of his editorial and political career. His entrance into partisan politics also forced Greeley to confront the emerging debate over slavery and the politics of class. As he grappled with these issues, Greeley began to probe the radical potentials and see the liberal limitations of his ideology. For the 1830s, Greeley's Whiggery thus provides the best illustration of the politics of reform in nineteenth-century America.

I

Jacksonian politics began in the presidential election of 1824. The War of 1812 had effectively destroyed the Federalist Party and with it the first American party system. The next decade, often portrayed as the "Era of Good Feelings," witnessed the one-party rule of the National Republicans, followers of Thomas Jefferson and James Madison. With no opposition party, the National Republicans split into factions based both on sections and personalities. The use of the congressional caucus, a small group of party leaders in Congress, for choosing presidential candidates came under increasing attack. In 1824, five candidates sought the presidency: John C. Calhoun of South Carolina, William H. Crawford of Georgia, Andrew Jackson of Tennessee, Henry Clay of Kentucky, and John Quincy Adams of Massachusetts. When no candidate received a majority of the electoral vote in the presidential canvass, the election went to the House of Representatives to decide. Clay, the Speaker of the House, told his supporters to throw their support to Adams, who eventually was elected president. When President Adams appointed Clay as his secretary of state (often seen as a stepping-stone to the presidency), angry critics accused the two of a "corrupt bargain." This charge, never conclusively proven, alienated Calhoun and enraged Jackson, who vowed to defeat Adams in 1828.

As president, John Quincy Adams failed to develop the political base and party apparatus necessary to sustain his administration. Promoting a sweeping program of internal improvements that included art and science, Adams alienated many former Jeffersonians. Two contending factions soon emerged: Adams, Clay, and the National Republicans on one side, and a new Democratic Party centered around Andrew Jackson on the other. The true party leader of the Democrats was Martin Van Buren, head of the powerful "Albany Regency" political machine in New York. Recognizing the necessities of a new partisan politics, Van Buren forged a coalition between the "plain Republicans of the North" and the planters of the South. The Democrats also enlisted westerners opposed to Clay and former Federalists in New York and New Jersey. In anticipation of the presidential election in 1828, Van Buren and his followers created a potent partisan political force of editors and local Democratic machines. "Outmanoeuvred on every side," Greeley recalled in his autobiography, "we were clearly foredoomed to defeat." Andrew Jackson won in a lopsided victory.

Henry Clay was a leading Whig idol of Greeley's. (Courtesy of the Library of Congress)

The Whig Party to which Horace Greeley would become so passionately attached was essentially formed in opposition to Jackson. Three events generally defined the Jacksonian presidency: Indian removal, nullification, and the Bank War.

In 1830, Jacksonians in Congress passed a removal bill that forced Native Americans of the Five Civilized Tribes to leave their ancestral lands in the Southeast and relocate to the Oklahoma Indian Reserve. In so doing, Jackson strengthened his connection with expansionist Southern planters and appeased states' rights advocates in Georgia. Indian removal also laid the foundation for a Democratic alliance with racism and generated humanitarian protest among evangelical clergymen who would become important allies of the Whig Party.

In the nullification controversy, Jackson paradoxically took a more nationalistic stand. During the late 1820s, South Carolina suffered an economic downturn. Disgruntled cotton planters blamed the federal tariff. Material discontent found theoretical expression in the constitutional arguments of John C. Calhoun, who asserted that a state could nullify a federal law it deemed unconstitutional. In 1832, states' rights radicals, followers of Calhoun, succeeded in calling a convention in South Carolina that nullified the 1828 tariff. To preserve the integrity of the Union, Jackson not only threatened military force but personally vowed to go down to the Palmetto State and hang Calhoun (his former vice president!). Cooler heads fortunately prevailed, and a compromise tariff engineered by Henry Clay diffused the nullification controversy. After this so-called Compromise of 1833, Greeley recalled, "the land had peace again for a brief season." Yet it bespoke the problem of minority rights in a democracy and raised the specter of disunion as a defense against majority rule.

The Bank War in particular defined Jacksonism and hence laid the ideological foundations for the opposition Whig Party. Chartered in 1816, the Second Bank of the United States (BUS) acted as a repository for government tax receipts and handled the financial affairs of the federal government. The bank became a powerful institution under the stewardship of Nicholas Biddle of Philadelphia and generated opposition among several groups in the Jacksonian coalition. Some Democrats associated with smaller state banks resented the power of Biddle's bank. Other Democrats, such as presidential advisors Amos Kendall and Francis Blair, were more attached to the principle of hard money; they argued that only specie (gold or silver) should serve as currency.

In a political move designed to hurt Jackson in the 1832 election, Clay and Daniel Webster pushed through Congress a bill rechartering the BUS for another twenty years. In July, the president vetoed the bill with a stinging message that pitted the democratic

people against the aristocratic special interests represented by
the bank. After winning another mandate in the fall presidential
contest, Jackson pursued a hard-money policy by removing federal
deposits from the BUS and transferring them to state banks. His
actions pitted him in a dramatic confrontation with Biddle, who
proceeded to call in the BUS's loans to smaller banks. As a good
Whig, Greeley believed that the fault lay with Jackson's "imperious
will." The effects of this so-called Bank War reverberated through
the economy and politics of the late 1830s and early 1840s.

II

Not unlike their Democratic counterparts, the Whigs were a combination of different groups and interests. Many, such as Henry
Clay, emerged from divisions within the Jeffersonian Republicans.
They tended to be those Jeffersonians with nationalist inclina-
tions who had supported presidents Madison and Monroe in their
expansion of governmental power. Opposition to the Jacksonian
Democrats also came from former Anti-Masons and states' rights
Southerners who were angry with Jackson for his stance against the
nullifiers. During the early years of the Whig Party, the unification
of Anti-Masons and National Republicans would prove particularly
challenging. Opposition leaders like Clay and Webster waited for
the Jacksonian coalition to disintegrate, yet they underestimated
the power of Jackson's charismatic leadership.

The Bank War provided the opportunity to bring together the
disparate strands of Jacksonian opposition. By mid-December 1833,
anti-Jackson forces had taken control of key Senate committees and
thus became a congressional party worthy of partisan status. Whig
leaders in Washington used the *National Intelligencer*, which had
served as the semi-official voice of the Adams administration, as an
important bond of political cohesion.

National Whigs based their opposition to Jackson on the
grounds of executive tyranny. The name "Whig" referred to the
opposition of American Revolutionaries to the tyrannical power of
King George III. Greeley recalled that the Whigs took their name

"to indicate their repugnance to unauthorized assumptions of Executive power." He recognized that various groups joined together with new voters angered "by the palpable usurpations of the Executive." Throughout the 1830s, Whigs hammered away at Jackson for what they saw as an unwarranted expansion of executive authority. Greeley often attacked Jackson and Van Buren for demagoguery and abuse of power, urging limits on the "Patronage of the Federal Executive." He maintained that executive patronage "now poisons the fountains of political power." Whigs also drew attention to Jackson's use of the "spoils system," in which government jobs went to partisan political supporters.

Henry Clay served as the titular head of the Whig Party until his death in 1852. Born in Virginia, Clay migrated to Kentucky, where he rose quickly in political and social circles. A committed Jeffersonian Republican, he filled an unexpired term in the U.S. Senate in 1806. Clay later became Speaker of the House of Representatives and was one of the "War Hawks," a faction of young Republicans that pushed the Madison administration toward the War of 1812. He then helped negotiate the Treaty of Ghent, which ended this inconclusive conflict with Great Britain. As mentioned earlier, Clay served as secretary of state under President John Quincy Adams. He earned his sobriquet of the "Great Compromiser" during the Missouri crisis of 1819–1820 and again during the nullification controversy.

Yet it was as the author of the "American System" that Clay became an ideological founder of the Whig Party. Clay was an economic nationalist who believed that government should promote economic growth through banks, internal improvements, and tariffs. Greeley presented Clay as "eminently National in his views and feelings, a leading champion of Internal Improvements, Protection to Home Industry, and good work." Clay's goal, shared with Whigs like Greeley, was an economically diverse nation with agriculture, commerce, and manufacturing leaning upon and reinforcing one another.

For many Whigs, Henry Clay was a larger-than-life figure who embodied the Whig vision of American republicanism. On his first visit to Washington, Greeley saw Clay in Congress, observing, "The

most striking person on the floor is Mr. Clay, who is incessantly
in motion, and whose spare, erect form betrays an easy dignity ap-
proaching to majesty, and a perfect gracefulness, such as I have
never seen equaled." Throughout his life, Greeley remained a devoted follower of Clay's and saw the Whig Party as the institutionalization of Clay's policies and values.

Throughout the 1830s and 1840s, state politics were of vital
importance in shaping the Whig Party. With the national impetus
from Washington, Whigs across the nation simultaneously formed
party organizations on the state level. Indeed, Horace Greeley devoted much of his editorial and political labors to Whig affairs in
New York. The Whig Party in the Empire State followed a similar
trajectory as the national organization. In 1830, supporters of Clay
met in New York City to make plans for "a party in opposition to
the general administration." Thurlow Weed, a former Anti-Mason
and editor of the Albany *Evening Journal*, was an early architect of
the New York Whigs. For the election of 1832, he worked to unite
Anti-Masons and National Republicans on common electoral tick-
ets. Yet his efforts proved stillborn as Jackson swept the state and
the Democratic candidate for governor won a narrow victory.

Whigs in New York made further steps toward organization in
1833 and 1834. Like the national party, New York Whigs were an
amalgam of groups hostile to Jackson and New York Democratic
leader Martin Van Buren. Once again, issues over banking provided
the spark to party organization. The harmful effects of the Bank
War were especially visible in New York City, the commercial
center of the country and a rival to Philadelphia, where the BUS
was located. Public meetings were held throughout the city. The
municipal elections of 1834 were closely watched to gauge the
strength of anti-Jackson opposition. Whig editor Hezekiah Niles,
whose *Niles' Weekly Register* (founded in Baltimore in 1811) advocated for protectionism, believed that trends in New York revealed
a change "in the political opinions of the people of this state,
or there is new zeal to give them effect." During this campaign,
Greeley edited a campaign newspaper called the *Constitution*. The
Democrats won the election for mayor of New York City, but Whigs
elected a majority of the Common Council.

In September 1834, New York Whigs met in a state convention to nominate William Henry Seward for governor. Even though Seward was defeated, New York Whigs had taken crucial steps toward partisan organization. At the state level, a Whig State Central Committee directed policy. County and district committees and conventions attended to politics at more local levels. By 1837, profiting from economic hard times, the Whigs were able to capture a majority in the New York State Assembly.

In the 1836 presidential race, the Democrats nominated Jackson's handpicked successor, Martin Van Buren. Nationally, the Whigs failed to decide on a single candidate, so different candidates were supported in different regions: William Henry Harrison of Indiana in the West, Hugh Lawson White of Tennessee in the Southwest, Daniel Webster in New England, and Willie P. Mangum in the Southeast. Looking back, Greeley claimed that he was "among the very few in the Eastern States who had taken any interest in bringing forward General Harrison as a candidate, believing that there was the raw material for a good run in his history

Greeley supports Clay for the Whig presidential nomination before the 1848 convention. (Courtesy of the Library of Congress)

and character." Although Van Buren won the electoral vote hand-
ily, Whigs had seen the potential popularity of Harrison. "In that
slouching Whig defeat of 1836," Greeley maintained, "lay the germ
of the overwhelming Whig triumph of 1840."

III

The essential differences between Whigs and Democrats rested
upon distinctive and opposing responses to the rise of a market
economy and society. As historian Lawrence Kohl explains, "The
era's great political division between Democrats and Whigs largely
reflected the division between those Americans who were deeply
unsettled by the emergence of an individualistic social order and
those whose character structure allowed them to strive more confidently within it." In general, Whigs like Greeley welcomed the
changes wrought by economic modernization. They believed that
the capitalist transformation would bring more freedom and liberty
and that the American nation should develop through time rather
than expand geographically across space. They insisted that government and other institutions could facilitate progress. Kohl has suc-
cinctly and accurately described the Whig persuasion as a "world
of contracts and constitutions, corporations and voluntary associations." Accordingly, the Whig Party appealed to those Americans
more fully engaged in a market economy: businessmen, merchants,
manufacturers, artisans, wealthy Southern planters growing staples
for exports, and cash-crop farmers.

Whig economic theory rested on the acceptance of capitalism
and its concomitant social structure and values. "Industry—" Greeley once wrote, "universal, well-directed, preserving industry—is
the breeze which must bear the good ship Public Weal off the
threatening breakers of bankruptcy and ruin." During the economic
downturn of the late 1830s, Greeley maintained that speculation "is
not an evil of itself, but the contrary, and relieves public distress
far oftener than it creates it." Whigs such as Greeley saw harmony
rather than conflict governing the economic sphere. Rather than

class conflict, Whigs stressed the essential compatibility between labor and capital.

The fundamental tenets of Whig economic theory were perhaps best represented by Henry C. Carey, whose articles were often reprinted in Greeley's *Tribune*. Carey assumed the basic compatibility among free enterprise, economic development, and social stability. Like all Whigs, he claimed that government has a role in aiding development. Carey also lauded the fluidity of the capitalist order, insisting that the wage-earning class would not pose a danger as long as there was opportunity for mobility.

Throughout the 1830s, Horace Greeley subscribed to the economic tenets of Whiggery. He embraced the dynamic nature of capitalist development: "Revolution, Progress, Change, Improvement, are as necessary in the political as in the natural world." Characteristically, he described his political allies as "the friends of good government, of enlightened policy and of National prosperity and virtue." Unlike their Democratic opponents who wanted to limit the role of government, Whigs like Greeley saw a positive role for state activism. "We have been accustomed," he wrote in 1839, "to regard Government not as a mere league for mutual defence against aggression and flagrant wrong, but as an association to secure good as well as to prevent evil—not only to preclude or punish injuries but to devise benefits. We regard a State or Nation as an association of the people of a certain district for whatever desirable purposes may be more easily and effectively subserved in their joint [rather] than their individual capacity."

Internal improvements were central to Whig economic thinking. "It is now fully decided," Greeley wrote in 1836, "that the improvement of the State by affording the greatest possible facilities to commercial intercourse is a settled and prominent feature of our policy, to be urged forward or delayed as circumstances shall dictate, but never to be lost sight of until ultimately successful." He expressed similar views in an editorial from the *New-Yorker* that urged the multiplication and improvement of channels of communication "and in every way give a stimulus to industry and enterprise."

Banking was perhaps the most pressing economic issue divid-
ing Democrats and Whigs. Jackson and his hard-money advocates
were generally hostile to banks. In particular, Jacksonian Democrats opposed large institutions like the national BUS, which in
their view were created for the interests of the propertied few. In
contrast, Whigs supported banks as essential institutions in a capitalist economy. In his autobiography, Greeley recalled that he had
always been "a zealous, determined advocate of a National Bank."
He insisted that state acts that incorporated banks were in principle
"emphatically politic, unexceptionable, and republican."

Throughout the 1830s, Greeley wrote many articles in defense
of banking. A *New-Yorker* editorial titled "Banks and the Producing
Classes" was aimed at workingmen. Acknowledging that paper currency and the credit system were under attack in 1836, he nonetheless defended their wisdom: "Who does not know that the general
influence of the Credit System on the business, currency, and
enterprise of the nation has never been more pervading, unshaken,
and beneficent [than] at this moment?" Greeley refuted the idea
that banking was class legislation aimed to benefit the wealthy at
the expense of the producing classes. He insisted that capital and
labor were "mutually dependent on each other for prosperity and
usefulness." Unintentionally anticipating his future involvement
with utopian socialism, Greeley explained further that "Capital is
Labor already performed, while Labor is Capital now being or about
to be realized."

Greeley penned another editorial for farmers. He maintained
that farmers benefited from the widespread existence of credit—
their most desirable state was that in which agricultural surplus
would bring in the highest returns. The Whig editor warned farmers
that an overthrow of the banking and credit system would "infal-
libly, from its inevitable effort of rendering money far less plenti-
ful and enhancing exorbitantly the actual rates of interest, prove
disastrous to all classes of producers, and none more emphatically
than those who cultivate the soil." Greeley also cautioned farmers
against any alliance with "the mustering legions of Agrarianism," a
reference to a Whiggish fear of economic leveling.

New York Whigs supported the democratization of banking through the New York General Banking Law of 1838 (sometimes called the Free Banking Act). The leaders of the New York Democracy, especially the Albany Regency, had ties to the existing state banking system. The Whigs wanted to create more opportunities for banking. Skillfully co-opting radical Democratic demands for bank reform, William H. Seward proposed a bill that would essentially end the Democratic practice of special bank charters through legislative lobbying. "It is intended," Greeley explained, "to obviate the necessity of any special legislative grant of Bank Charters or Banking privileges in all time hereafter." Individuals who met minimum requirements of capitalization of federal and state bonds would automatically receive incorporation as a bank. Greeley considered the "Free Banking System" to be a "great and admirable improvement on the corrupting political monopoly it superseded" and hoped that the "public mind—not of the rash, the restless and the fickle, but of the sedate, the reflecting, the intelligent—is nearly ripe for this step."

Whigs argued that an ample supply of sound currency would facilitate commercial relations and economic growth. For Whigs, this meant paper money like banknotes. Greeley recalled in his autobiography that he had always been an advocate of an "abundant currency," explaining that any expedient "by which a cheap currency may be substituted for an expensive one, effects a savings for the public." Believing that the scarcity of money before 1830 had "palsied enterprise and petrified labor," Greeley supported an elastic currency system that included gold, silver, and paper money furnished by banks. Like most Whigs, he feared that the hard-money policy of the Jacksonians would destroy the credit system. Thus, Whigs opposed the Jackson administration's Specie Circular, an 1836 measure that curtailed the use of paper money by requiring payment for public lands in hard coin (specie) only.

Banking and currency were not the only issues that generated partisan strife between Whigs and Democrats. In 1836, Congress passed the Deposit-Distribution Act, calling for the distribution of the current treasury surplus to the states to build roads and canals. "Distribution" was a cause long advanced by Henry Clay and the

Whigs, for it spoke to the national desire for internal improvements. Greeley supported distribution, explaining in an April 1836 editorial that the existence of a surplus put the United States in a unique and advantageous position.

While president, John Quincy Adams had intended to use the surplus for "the construction of works of great and acknowledged public utility." But this surplus was lost in the Panic of 1837 and subsequent economic depression. Whigs proposed to combat the depression with more paper money, but Democratic president Martin Van Buren announced his Subtreasury, or Independent Treasury, plan in 1837, which aimed at separating government finance from the banks. Greeley opposed the Independent Treasury idea as an embodiment of radical Democratic hard-money policy, insisting that the plan was "revolutionary in its character, despotic in its tendency, and destructive to the prosperity and advancement of our country." A reduction of circulating medium would reduce prices of property and commodities and push those in debt into bankruptcy. Greeley warned his readers not to be seduced by Democratic rhetoric. Fighting for the mantle of Jeffersonian republicanism, Greeley maintained that "nearly every family which was prominent for the devotion of its members to the Democratic cause from 1800 to 1812 is equally prominent now in its hostility to the Sub-Treasury projects and party."

Land was another economic issue that generated partisan strife in the early nineteenth century. During the 1820s, the land question was framed as a sectional issue. In general, the western states wanted cheap land to encourage settlement, while manufacturers in the eastern states were fearful that it would drain off their labor supply. Democrat Thomas Hart Benton of Missouri supported what was known as "graduation," reducing the price of public land until it found a buyer. Greeley opposed Democratic plans for preemption and graduation. "We doubt the policy of restricting the sale of land to actual settlers," he warned in a *New-Yorker* editorial of December 1836.

The Whig alternative, embodied in Henry Clay's Distribution Bill, allowed the federal government to distribute the proceeds of public land sales to the states according to population for purposes of internal improvements, education, and colonization. Clay's distribution plan was a compromise effort that offered westerners guaranteed subsidies for internal improvements and easterners a security against destabilization of the land system. Distribution soon became part of Whig economic policy. Whigs maintained that the western domain could be used as a capital fund, a source of revenue to finance internal improvements. Clay's Distribution Bill passed the Congress in 1833, but was vetoed by President Jackson.

The plan came up again in 1836. "It is the view of Mr. Clay," Greeley explained, "that the National Domain is thus vested in the General Government as a species of trust property, to be managed for the best common interest of the States for which it is held in trust, and with strict reference to the original terms of the trust." In other words, the public lands "constitute an immense trust fund, which may be profligately squandered, to the infinite detriment of the original States, or be employed under wise and provident regulations for the common and permanent benefit of the Union." In 1838, Greeley offered to write an article on public lands for the Whig *American Monthly Magazine* on the belief that the subject could be a great card for the Whigs in the older states of the East "if judiciously handled and forcibly presented."

Greeley's views on land, currency, and banking closely reflected Whig economic philosophy. Yet the local context also shaped Greeley's response to economic questions. Editing newspapers in New York City, Greeley witnessed the emerging workingmen's movements of the early 1830s. Beginning in 1833, rapid inflation and a rise in commodity prices were fomenting discontent among urban workers. In response, journeymen and wage earners formed the General Trades' Union and engaged in strikes. Workingmen were at the forefront of labor protest during this decade and pioneered an ideological assault on free market capitalism. They attacked monopolies, claiming that "the *employer* was rapidly running the road to wealth [while] the *employed* was too often the victim of poverty and oppression, bound to the vassalage of inadequate award for his labor."

Beginning in 1828, urban workers began to organize "workingmen's" parties in such cities as Philadelphia, New York, and Boston.

In 1834, radical workingmen in New York formed the Equal Rights Party. At one meeting, conservative Democrats tried to silence these workers by turning off the gaslights. Having been warned in advance, however, the prepared workingmen lit the room with matches called "locofocos." The name soon became synonymous with radical, anti-monopolistic Democrats. Locofocos ran their own candidate, Alexander Ming, for mayor in 1836.

Greeley often denounced what he saw as radical agrarianism among the New York workingmen. In an attack on Orestes Brownson's "The Laboring Classes" (1840), he argued that Locofocism was "utterly Subversive of all Rights of Property whatever." The growing organization, militancy, and class consciousness of New York's workingmen help account for the thread of conservatism that runs through Greeley's writings of the 1830s. It surfaced, for example, in the editorial "Democracy—What Is It?" that appeared in the *Jeffersonian* in May 1838. Having first divorced the term from the name of a contemporary political party, he explained that democracy "imports that all men 'are of right free and equal'—not equal in worldly advantages, nor in physical perfection—in wealth or in beauty—in moral worth nor in intellectual power." Greeley then added an important qualification on equality, one that appeared often in the writings of American Whigs: "Every one knows that in knowledge, in virtue, in fidelity, in honor, as in fortune, in strength, in height, men differ as do in size the trees of the forest or the fish of the ocean." Despite this caveat about equality, Greeley affirmed the association between democracy and popular sovereignty. As a fundamental truth, democracy maintains "that each member of a community shall have a fair, free and equal voice in the making or changing of those laws by which that community is governed." Greeley explained further that the "great axiom" of democracy was the insistence "that a majority of all those to be affected by a political or municipal regulation shall first give their consent to its enactment, and that without this its enforcement is tyranny and usurpation."

Throughout the 1830s and 1840s, Whigs like Greeley remained suspicious of what they saw as the "leveling" tendencies of the Democrats. Instead, Whigs posed as defenders of property rights and the principle of law as a means of social order and communal unity.

IV

The ideology of the Whig Party was moral as well as economic. In his newspapers, Whig leader Thurlow Weed supported a variety of humanitarian reforms, such as temperance, ending imprisonment for debt, and laws against usury. Whigs generally took an organic view of society that accepted inequalities as natural and inevitable. They saw improvement in terms of social order and individual self-control. Not surprisingly, Whigs were leaders behind such institutions as voluntary associations and schools. In partisan contrast, Democrats wanted to strengthen the barrier between the private and public. In the Jacksonian era, they were the ones who fought for the separation between church and state. Greeley's involvement in the moral reforms of the period, treated more fully in the next chapter, is illustrated in his views on education.

In 1838, Greeley stated that "the cause of Education is the personal concern of every man who has any thing to hope or fear from the future. It is the sheet-anchor of the universal and necessary faith of all men that the rights of property will always be respected by the community, and that the indigent as a class will never unite to better their condition by the systematic and legalized plunder of the wealthy." Like most Whigs, Greeley saw the expansion of schools as a part of modernization. "Education," he explained, "is designed to train up youth to a more advantageous employment both of their mental and physical powers in advancement of the welfare of the community and themselves."

Greeley warned that schools had been lax in their responsibilities as moral guardians. Reflecting the conservative and paternalistic assumptions of Whiggery, Greeley insisted that "happiness is only to be found in obedience to those laws which a wise and beneficent Creator has appointed for the government of human conduct." He closed by calling for "greater facilities for the instruction of competent

Teachers" and common school libraries, revealingly labeling them "an Association for Intellectual and Moral Improvement."

V

The 1830s were a critical turning point in the slavery controversy in America. During the first three decades of the nineteenth century, colonization was the most popular solution to the problem of slavery. Eminent statesmen like Supreme Court Justice John Marshall and Henry Clay supported the plan to free the slaves and send them back to Africa through private voluntary contributions. Several events around 1830 augured a new militant abolitionism that challenged the inherent injustice of colonization. In 1829, free black David Walker of Boston published his *Appeal to the Colored Citizens of the World*, a revolutionary call for slaves to rise up and seize their freedom. On January 1, 1831, William Lloyd Garrison published the first issue of the *Liberator*. Promising not to retreat a single inch and to be heard, Garrison launched the movement of immediate abolitionism—the notion that slavery was a sin that should be abolished immediately and without compensation to slaveholders. In August of that same year, Nat Turner led a slave revolt in Southampton County, Virginia, that left fifty-seven whites dead.

By 1833, an American Anti-Slavery Society had been formed. Local organizations sprouted up across the Northeast and Midwest. In 1835, the abolitionists launched a postal campaign to flood the South with antislavery literature. Brothers Arthur and Lewis Tappan and Gerrit Smith spread abolitionism through New York State. In October 1835, the New York State Antislavery Society was founded. The rise of militant abolitionism sparked violent opposition among a population deeply imbued with racism and fearful of social disorder. That year anti-abolition riots broke out in various places, including Boston, New York, and Canterbury, Connecticut.

As an emerging newspaper editor and Whig politico, Horace Greeley could not ignore this important transformation from colonization to abolitionism. He closely followed the growing debate over slavery in national councils and noted the progress of the abolitionist movement. During the 1830s, Greeley clearly voiced his opposition to slavery, though he failed to embrace abolitionism. He later recalled that "while I could not withhold from these agitators a certain measure of sympathy for their great and good object, I was utterly unable to see how their efforts tended to the achievement of their end."

The slavery issue also arose with the birth of the Texas Republic. On March 2, 1836, fifty-eight Texans led by Sam Houston signed a declaration of independence from Mexico. A little more than a month later, Texans defeated Mexican troops at San Jacinto. Greeley supported the cause of Texas freedom, describing it as "a gallant and effectual blow . . . for the cause of political liberty and religious toleration." Many Americans saw in the Texas struggle a mirror of their own revolutionary crusade against Great Britain and applauded the Protestant struggle against Catholic Mexico. Reflecting these views, Greeley extended his sympathy with Texans "in their exultation at the downfall of the tyrant, and their deliverance from the sway of narrow-minded rapacity, benighted bigotry, and a bloody military despotism." After declaring their independence, Texans hoped to join the United States.

While the debate over the annexation of Texas would not fully unfold until the 1840s, Greeley early on opposed annexation because he did not want to see Texas—which had been populated by Southerners—become another slave state. Moreover, it went against "our own cherished principle of non-intervention in the affairs of other nations." Annexation would also tarnish the image of the United States in the world. "Our territory is already ample," Greeley explained, "our maritime frontier one of unprecedented extent, yet at all points assailable and inviting—our conflicting interests so numerous and weighty that we shall be fortunate indeed if the virtue of our people and the wisdom and moderation of our rulers shall suffice to preserve the integrity of the Union for a century longer." Already in the 1830s, Greeley articulated what would become a standard Whig refrain against Democratic territorial expansionism.

On November 7, 1837, antislavery editor Elijah Lovejoy was murdered in Alton, Illinois, while defending his press from an anti-abolitionist mob. "Lovejoy was deliberately, systematically, hunted to his death," Greeley recalled, "simply because he would not, in a nominally Free State, cease to bear testimony as a Christian minister and journalist to the essential iniquity of slaveholding. It was thenceforth plain to my apprehension, that Slavery and true Freedom could not coexist on the same soil." By vividly exposing the danger of violent interference with free speech in Jacksonian America, Lovejoy's martyrdom became a celebrated cause in the movement for abolition.

The contest between slavery and freedom would occupy Greeley throughout his public life. He would become one of the leaders in the Republican Party, founded to halt the spread of slavery into the territories. During the Civil War, Greeley would join with the Radical faction of the Republican Party that pushed for wartime emancipation.

In his autobiographical *Recollections of a Busy Life*, Greeley reconstructed his evolution toward abolitionism with accuracy and a little hindsight. Despite his conflicted relationship with President Abraham Lincoln during the war, he acknowledged that Lincoln "forcibly gave expression to what was the very general experience of American boys reared in the Free States forty to sixty years ago, while the traditions and the impulses of our Revolutionary age were still vivid and pervading,—at least, of those trained by intelligent Federal mothers."

Perhaps eager to establish his antislavery credentials, Greeley recalled that during the Missouri Controversy, when he was only seven years old, he "intensely sympathized with the North in her effort to prevent the admission of Missouri as a Slave State." Yet he explains in his autobiography why he was not an abolitionist: "Conservative by instinct, by tradition, and disinclined to reject or leave undone the practical good within reach, while straining after the ideal good that was clearly unattainable, I clung fondly to the Whig party, and deprecated the Abolition or Third Party movement in politics, as calculated fatally to weaken the only great National organization which was likely to oppose an effective resistance to the persistent exactions and aggressions of the Slave Power."

Greeley's writings during the 1830s testify to some antislavery, though not abolitionist, credentials. In 1834, he argued that the

Founding Fathers were right not to interfere with the question of domestic slavery: "Why should not even the existing evils of one section be left to the correction of its own wisdom and virtue, when pointed out by the unerring finger of experience?" Greeley also supported colonization, explaining that "if the African race are ever to be raised to a degree of comparative happiness, intelligence, and freedom, it must be in some other region than that which has been the theater of their servitude and degradation." Perhaps influenced by the course of events, Greeley had become more vocal in his criticisms of slavery later in the decade. "Democracy and Slavery," he wrote in 1838, "are ideas wholly incompatible. They cannot assimilate; they are antipodes." Greeley raised this inconsistency while discussing Virginia, a slave society with "an aristocratic temperament and bearing." If Virginia was considered a democratic order, as some mistakenly claimed, "then it is high time we had new authorities for the meaning of language."

VI

For Horace Greeley, the 1830s marked more than his initiation into the politics of Whiggery and antislavery. It marked as well his introduction to the institution of marriage. Greeley was living in a Graham boardinghouse in New York, a residence based upon the dietary prescriptions of Sylvester Graham, father of the still-famous Graham cracker: whole wheat bread, fresh fruits and vegetables, fibrous cereals, and fresh drinking water. Here Greeley met Mary ("Molly") Youngs Cheney from Connecticut, a schoolteacher with an active mind. Margaret Fuller recalled that Mary was "crazy for learning." Greeley and Cheney were married on July 5, 1836, in Warrenton, North Carolina, where Mary had been teaching at a private school. It was the only time, Greeley noted, that he ever wore silk stockings. The wedding reception was held at the home of William Bragg, whose son Braxton would achieve fame as a Confederate general. Greeley was twenty-five and Mary twenty-two.

The Greeleys moved to 124 Green Street, close both to the offices of the *New-Yorker* and to New York City Hall. Soon their marriage was beset by health problems and conflicts that would

continue to torment their relationship. By most accounts, it was
not a happy match. In August 1838, their first son died at birth.
In December 1839, Greeley wrote to a friend that Mary was still
"terribly ill and down-hearted" from the miscarriage. She also came
down with dyspepsia, a digestive ailment no doubt caused by anxiety. The Greeleys did share some kind of intellectual companion-
ship, for they both explored the writings of the Transcendentalists.
Yet Mary would become depressed and irritable as Greeley worked
long hours with the additional travel time from New York to Albany
covering state politics. He seemed unable to give her the kind of attention she needed. No doubt the idiosyncratic Greeley was not an
easy person to live with, but Mary became for him a lifelong burden
both emotionally and physically.

VII

A year after their marriage, Greeley had to face problems other than
domestic ones. In 1837, the United States was hit with a severe
financial panic and depression that stretched into the early 1840s.
Rooted in the speculative frenzy of the 1830s, the panic began
when New York City banks suspended specie payments in May
1837. Other banks followed suit, calling in outstanding loans and
cutting off credit. Although the panic followed a boom period of
speculation in canals and railroads, Greeley, in good Whig fashion,
blamed the Democrats. Jackson's Specie Circular, he declared, had
"precipitated the catastrophe it was intended to avert."

The Panic of 1837 hit all classes. The propertied elite felt the
depression of land values, while laborers suffered from unemploy-
ment. "Manufactories were stopped, and their 'hands' thrown out of
work," Greeley recalled. "Trade was almost stagnant. Bankruptcies
among men of business were rather the rule than the exception.
Property was sacrificed at auction—often at sheriff's or assignee's
sale—for a fraction of its value; and thousands, who had fondly
dreamed themselves millionaires, or on the point of becoming such,
awoke to the fact that they were bankrupt." Greeley was also moved
by the human suffering he saw around him in New York, people liv-

ing in "damp, narrow cellars, or rickety, wretched tenements, unfit for cleanly brutes."

The Depression of 1837 sharpened partisan conflict across the nation. As the party in power, the Democrats suffered more from the politics of depression. The national party split over financial policies into hard-money and soft-money wings. President Van Buren aligned himself with the hard-money, anti-banking, Locofoco faction of the Democratic Party. A group that became known as Conservative Democrats, including New York's Senator Nathaniel Tallmadge and Representative John C. Clark, broke with the hard-money trend of the party. They established their own newspaper in Washington, the *Madisonian*. Some Conservative Democrats even joined the Whig Party. In New York, William H. Seward urged Whigs in the state legislature to support the reelection of Tallmadge to the Senate.

The economic depression proved to be a valuable boost for the Whig Party, as Democratic financial policies were easier targets to attack. The Whigs, now able to pose as the friends of economic prosperity, defined themselves more sharply along the economic issues set forth by Greeley and others. They campaigned against Democratic fiscal policies, claiming that they were responsible for the scarcity of currency in New York.

Anticipating the state campaign in 1838, Thurlow Weed, editor of the Albany *Evening Journal* and a leading architect of the state and national Whig parties, approached Greeley. "In casting about for an editor," Weed later recalled, "it occurred to me that there was some person connected with the *New Yorker*, a literary journal published in that city, possessing the qualities needed for our new enterprise . . . a strong tariff man, and probably an equally strong Whig." Greeley recalled similarly: "To maintain and confirm the Whig ascendancy, it had been resolved to publish, throughout 1838, a cheap weekly journal to be called the Jeffersonian, which I had been pitched upon as the proper person to edit." Weed offered Greeley a thousand dollars for the job, which obliged him to spend over half his time in Albany.

Greeley edited the *Jeffersonian* from February 1838 through February 1839. In the morning, he would go to the State Assembly in Albany to gather news. In the afternoon, he returned to his boardinghouse room, where he would work on the newspaper. Henry J. Raymond, later to become the editor of the *New York Times*, worked on the *Jeffersonian* as an editorial assistant. He claimed that Greeley worked quite hard, editing two newspapers (the *New-Yorker* as well) published in two different cities. The *Jeffersonian* contained political intelligence, speeches, and editorials. Designed "to convince and win by candor and moderation, rather than overbear by passion and vehemence," Greeley as editor sought to avoid "abuse, scurrility, and railing accusations." The circulation of the *Jeffersonian* reached about fifteen thousand. In no small part due to his efforts, the Whigs won a string of victories in New York in 1838. Seward won the gubernatorial election, beating sitting Democratic governor William L. Marcy by ten thousand votes. Whigs won a majority in the New York Assembly.

VIII

After a string of state and local victories in 1838, the Whigs looked ahead to the presidential election of 1840. Since the party now controlled the large and important state of New York, Weed was determined to play a key role in the Whig presidential nomination. Sensing victory, he did not want the Whigs to nominate Henry Clay. Weed and Seward realized that the former Mason would not be popular among former Anti-Masons. As a slaveholder, Clay would also alienate the growing number of abolitionists in New York. Weed wanted Greeley, his young editorial protégé, to go to Saratoga Springs, New York, in the summer of 1839 to meet with Clay and dissuade him from accepting the nomination in 1840. For reasons that remain unclear, Greeley never completed his political assignment.

Nor did the New York Whig leaders want the nomination to go to Daniel Webster, whose Federalist background and ties to Nicholas Biddle's Second Bank of the United States were serious liabilities. By the summer of 1839, Weed was pushing General Winfield Scott, a hero of the War of 1812, for the Whig nomination.

Whigs from across the country met in their first national convention in Harrisburg, Pennsylvania, in December 1839. Greeley attended this meeting as "a deeply interested observer." Yet, as part of the New York Whig Party, he did more than observe. In fact, Greeley's hotel room served as headquarters for the anti-Clay forces. After blocking Clay, Weed and Seward helped secure the nomination of William Henry Harrison, another military hero. Greeley believed that Harrison's "history and character" provided "the raw material for a good run." John Tyler of Virginia, the popular choice of Southern opponents of Van Buren, was chosen to run as vice president.

A strong national committee in Washington directed the Whig presidential campaign of 1840. It was assisted by state organizations and local Tippecanoe clubs. The Whig strategy was to present the presidential contest as a conflict between democratic and aristocratic ways of life. Drawing upon the anti-aristocratic rhetoric of their Jacksonian opponents, Whig politicos attempted to portray sitting president Martin Van Buren as an aristocrat who wore ruffled shirts, perfumed his whiskers, and ate from gold spoons. In his newspapers, Greeley reproduced articles that showed the pretentiousness and luxury of the Van Buren White House. One claimed that his extravagant chamber pot cost two dollars.

The Whigs also ran on their economic platform. They blamed Van Buren for the panic and depression, often calling the Democratic president "Martin Van Ruin." Like most Whigs, Greeley railed against the effects of Democratic economic policy, labeling the Democrats a "Shinplaster Party."

Active participation by women was a new departure in the Whig campaign of 1840. They attended conventions, cheered speakers, and rode in parade floats. In Fayette County, Illinois, Whig women gave a farewell celebration to delegates on their way to the state convention in Springfield. There were "Harrison ladies" in Roseville, Ohio, as well.

As a young but rapidly rising political journalist, Horace Greeley played a visible and influential role in the presidential election of 1840. He edited a campaign sheet, the *Log Cabin*, and published *Why I Am a Whig*. Once again, Greeley was editing two newspapers at once. "Writing for the common people," he explained, "I have aimed to be lucid and simple. I write for the great mass of intelligent, observant, reflecting farmers and mechanics, and if I succeed in making my positions clearly understood I do not fear that they will be rejected." Co-opting the populist rhetoric of Jacksonian Democrats, Greeley proclaimed in the first issue that the *Log Cabin* "will be a zealous and unwavering advocate of the rights, interests, and prosperity of our whole country, but especially those of the hardy subduers and cultivators of her soil. It will be the advocate of the cause of the Log Cabin against that of the Custom House and Presidential Palace." Following Whig strategy, Greeley also stressed the main Whig policies of a national bank, a tariff, and the distribution of the proceeds of public lands. He promised his readers that his newspaper would be "an advocate of Freedom, Improvement, and National Reform."

Perhaps Greeley's most noteworthy effort in the campaign of 1840 was to collect Whig campaign songs and publish them in the *Log Cabin Song Book*. Turning popular melodies into campaign parodies, Whig enthusiasts serenaded themselves with such songs as "Tippecanoe and Tyler Too," "Buckeye Cabin," and a "Tip-Top Song about Tippecanoe." "General Harrison," James Parton recalled, "was *sung* into the presidential chair."

Greeley admitted that the music was not very good, although he maintained that the songs attracted attention. Campaign songs were printed on the last page of each *Log Cabin*. In Greeley's eyes, each song was worth five hundred new subscribers. "Our songs," he wrote to Weed, "are doing more good than anything else." Reflecting much later upon the Whig victory of 1840, Greeley stated proudly that "we were far ahead of them in singing, and in electioneering emblems and mottoes which appealed to popular sympathies."

With both election platforms and platitudes, the *Log Cabin* was a successful campaign newspaper. Its circulation, which ran up to eighty thousand weekly, was "entirely beyond precedent." Fellow journalist Henry J. Raymond called Greeley's *Log Cabin* the most successful campaign newspaper ever published.

When the results came in, the Whigs had demonstrated their mastery of democratic electioneering. Harrison, who carried nineteen of twenty-six states, would become the first Whig president of the United States.

The Whig victory in 1840 clearly advanced the political and editorial fortunes of Greeley. "The man who contributed most to keep alive and increase the popular enthusiasm," insisted an early biographer, "the man who did most to feed that enthusiasm with the substantial fuel of fact and argument, was, beyond all question, Horace Greeley." With little modesty, Greeley agreed that "there were not many who had done more effective work in the canvass than I had."

IX

The 1830s might have been the most important decade in Greeley's life and career. It witnessed his move from the New England countryside to New York City, his marriage, his entry into Whig politics, and his initiation as a newspaper editor. Whiggery gave him the set of ideas that would guide him for the next three decades as he negotiated the politics of antislavery and responded to the class challenges of an urban industrial order. After the 1840 election, Horace Greeley had the confidence that he could edit an inexpensive Whig daily newspaper in New York City. This led him to found the *Tribune*, which would become one of the most influential journalistic endeavors of the nineteenth century.

Chapter Three

———————O———————

The World of Print Culture in Antebellum New York

IN HIS RECOLLECTIONS OF A BUSY LIFE, Horace Greeley dramatically expressed the hope "that the journal I projected and established will live and flourish long after I have shall mouldered into forgotten dust." Greeley, of course, was referring to the *New York Tribune*, the newspaper he founded in 1841 and edited (in some role or another) until his death in 1872. Greeley exerted his greatest influence on nineteenth-century America as editor of the *Tribune*. The newspaper had the largest circulation of any national newspaper of the era. During the 1850s, it had more than two hundred thousand readers and an average circulation of twenty-nine thousand. On the eve of the Civil War, the *Tribune* had forty-five thousand subscribers and an estimated audience of three hundred thousand. A contemporary journalist claimed that it was second only to the Bible throughout the West. Southern radical George Fitzhugh of Virginia, though no friend of the Republican *Tribune*, still acknowledged it as "the most . . . influential paper in the world." At Greeley's funeral, the eminent clergyman Henry Ward Beecher professed that there was "hardly an intelligent man or child that does not feel the influence of Horace Greeley."

The reputation of the *Tribune* extended beyond Greeley's lifetime. Historian James Ford Rhodes, who wrote at the turn of the twentieth century, remembered the *Tribune* as a "political Bible." It had the reputation of the kind of refined, intellectual journal similar to what the *New Republic* or *Atlantic Monthly* enjoys today. Clarence Darrow, the famous Chicago criminal lawyer, recalled that "as far back as I can remember, the *New York Tribune* was the political and social Bible of our home."

Greeley's position as editor was as—if not more—important than his role as reformer and politician. In early nineteenth-century America, the newspaper emerged as an institution that served political, intellectual, and even literary functions. A number of key American and European intellectuals—among them Albert Brisbane, Margaret Fuller, Mark Twain, and Karl Marx—crossed paths with the *Tribune* at some point in their careers. Greeley himself believed that his efforts at publishing a newspaper and advancing the cause of liberal reform and the interests of the Whig and Republican parties were complementary endeavors. Moreover, Greeley's newspapers became the vehicle through which he articulated and propagated his liberal Whiggish values. He both shaped and reflected the views of the Northern middle class on such issues as slavery and economic development. A recent student of the *New York Tribune* calls it a "key conceptual map" through which nineteenth-century Americans made sense of their world. For these reasons, let us pause and consider the history of Horace Greeley as a newspaper editor.

I

A communications revolution was central to the process of modernization in the early nineteenth-century United States. Internal improvements like steamboats, canals, and railroads vastly enhanced communications. Between 1815 and 1830, the number of post offices more than doubled. This striking advance in communications encouraged literary pursuits. Changes in printing, papermaking, and distribution rapidly increased the spread of print culture.

Magazine and newspaper publishing dramatically expanded from 1820 to 1850. By 1822, the United States had more newspapers than any other country in the world. In 1830, there were 650 weeklies and 65 daily papers published in America. A decade later, those numbers had grown to 1,141 weeklies and 138 dailies. There were seven major daily newspapers published in New York in 1835. In 1841, when Greeley started the *Tribune*, there were 100 periodicals published in the city and 12 daily papers. In 1855, there were 203 periodicals. This contributed, along with public education, to the creation of a new urban literate mass audience.

The rise of newspapers and other forms of print culture was closely tied to the growth of cities. In 1830, 8.8 percent of the U.S. population lived in urban areas. Two decades later, that percentage had risen to 15.2 percent. For several reasons, cities provided a receptive soil for the flowering of newspapers. Literacy rates tended to be higher than in rural areas. The nature of urban geography made it easier for a newspaper to reach a larger audience. New forms of urban leisure activities such as sports, theaters, museums, and lectures provided content for papers. In essence, the newspaper accompanied the rise of an urban middle class. It was this group that became a key audience for the *Tribune*, and it was for this group that Greeley crafted his ideas.

Technological changes also drove the rise of the newspaper in the early nineteenth century. A steam-driven, single-cylinder Napier press was capable of producing five thousand impressions per hour. Robert Hoe's "lightning press," first used in 1846, operated with enough cylinders to create twenty thousand impressions per hour by the 1850s. There were also changes in the production of paper. The Fourdrinier process transformed cotton rag pulp into paper, and new bleaching techniques allowed colored rags to be used in the manufacturing of paper. The newspaper industry was also aided by the increased speed of news transmission through the steamship, railroad, and telegraph. The first telegraph office opened in New York in January 1846. By 1854, the telegraph allowed for congressional debate to be read six hours later in the *Tribune*. In early 1849, a number of New York editors formed the Associated Press to rationalize and maximize the means of gathering news. This organized partnership leased telegraph lines and chartered a steamer from Halifax, where news from Europe first arrived.

The rise of the "penny press" was perhaps the most significant development in journalism in the Jacksonian era, providing an important precedent for Greeley's *Tribune*. By shunning partisan politics, increasing local news, and emphasizing sensational stories, the penny press marked a new direction in commercialization of the news. It was pioneered by Benjamin Day, who had served his journalistic apprenticeship in the workingmen's movement. In 1833, Day, using the newly invented cylinder press, began publishing the New York *Sun*. At the cost of one penny, it was far cheaper than the then-existing sixpenny papers. Aimed at a wide audience of artisans and workers, the *Sun* covered the daily lives of ordinary New Yorkers, along with sensational events like "fires, theatrical performances, elephants escaping from circus, [and] women trampled by hogs." Day's newspaper reported crime news by sending reporters to the police court. The penny press introduced other journalistic novelties as well. Revenue was secured from advertising, in which there apparently was little quality control. The *Sun*, for example, advertised any kind of patent medicines and even publicized the services of Madame Restell, one of New York's leading abortionists. It also engaged in hoaxes, like the 1835 articles on life on the moon presumably observed through a powerful new telescope. In another innovation, the penny paper was hawked in the streets by newsboys.

Within four months, the New York *Sun* had a circulation of four thousand. For a brief moment, it was the largest selling newspaper in the world. According to a leading historian of journalism, the penny press made "newspaper readers of a whole economic class which the six-cent dailies had scarcely touched." Poet Edgar Allan Poe believed that the penny press had an influence on American culture that was "probably beyond all calculation."

The rise of the penny press was closely related in New York and other cities to the workingmen's movement of the early 1830s. Newspapers like the *Workingmen's Advocate* and *Free Enquirer* served the needs of urban radicals and freethinkers. Benjamin Day had been part of a group of young editors who associated with radical reformers Robert Dale Owen and Frances Wright and the *Free Enquirer*. Workingmen's newspapers pioneered the techniques used by the penny press. Their goal was to create an ideological free market of ideas similar to the Jacksonian ideal of laissez-faire

Politics of antebellum New York journalism. (Courtesy of the Library of Congress)

economics. The working-class press helped spread democracy by diffusing knowledge among the urban population. The papers advocated the interests of wage earners and were generally supportive of the Democratic Party. According to historian Alexander Saxton, the penny press "propagated an urban artisan ideology that was rationalist and secular in tone, democratic in politics, expansionist in operation, and ferociously white egalitarian in its identification."

James Gordon Bennett's New York *Herald* succeeded the *Sun* as the most successful of the penny presses, dominating the newspaper market with about fifty-five thousand readers. The paper began in 1835 with an appeal to a mass audience: "Equally intended for the great masses of the community—the merchant, mechanic, working people—the private family as well as the public hotel—the journeyman and his employer—the clerk and his principal." It had a fleet of fast sailboats to get news from European steamers arriving in New York and was the first newspaper to send reporters to cover Washington. It was also the first to offer coverage of foreign news. The *Herald* promoted quality articles

about Wall Street, yet at the same time covered sensational murder trials like the one involving Helen Jewett, a prostitute found
killed. It was the first newspaper to make news of high society and
sent reporters to fancy balls.

II

On April 10, 1841, New Yorkers gathered for a funeral parade to
pay their respects to the recently deceased Whig president William
Henry Harrison. Despite the spring date, Greeley recalled that it
was "a day of most unseasonable chill and sleet and snow." He
remembered that day well for another reason: "On that leaden, fu-
nereal morning, the most inhospitable of the year, I issued the first
number of THE NEW YORK TRIBUNE."

Greeley had thought about a cheap Whig daily "addressed
more especially to the laboring class" that could compete with the
Democratic *Herald* and *Sun*. Yet he envisioned something more
than a mere partisan sheet: "I believe there was a happy medium
between these extremes,—a position from which a journal might
openly and heartily advocate the principles and commend the measures of that party to which his convictions allied him yet frankly
dissent from its course on a particular question, and even denounce
its candidates if they were shown to be deficient in capacity or (far
worse) in integrity." Following the success of the *Sun*, Greeley
aimed at producing a one-cent newspaper so that "the lawyer, the
merchant, the banker, the forwarder, the economist, the author,
the politician, etc., may find here whatever he needs to see, and
be spared the trouble of looking elsewhere." The Whiggish motto
on the masthead of the paper contained the reputed last words of
President William Henry Harrison: "I desire you to understand the
true principles of the government. I wish them carried out. I ask
nothing more."

Greeley set up shop for the *Tribune* at 30 Ann Street near
City Hall. Prominent New York Whig James Coggeshall lent him a
thousand dollars, while other political supporters gave him another
two thousand. The *Tribune* began with six hundred subscribers

and printed five thousand copies of the first edition. The paper's expenses for the first week were $525, while the receipts were just $92. The price of advertising was at first four cents a line but was quickly raised to six cents. The *Tribune* used carriers or newsboys who would sell the papers on the streets for a small profit. A companion *Weekly Tribune* began publication on September 2, 1841, with the subscription price of $2 per year.

In its early years, the *Tribune* employed about 120 people. By 1853, the newspaper had 13 editors and 183 employees. Thirty-eight correspondents sent in news; of these, twenty reported from foreign countries. Greeley hired Thomas McElrath as his business partner. "A strict disciplinarian, a close calculator, a man of method and order, experienced in business," James Parton recalled, "Mr. McElrath possessed in an eminent degree the very qualities in which the editor of the Tribune was most deficient." Greeley himself admitted that McElrath's business management "was so safe and judicious that it gave me no trouble, and scarcely required of me a thought, during that long era of all but unclouded prosperity." Greeley's reformist bent also shaped the *Tribune*'s management. In 1849, he and McElrath created the Tribune Association, a joint stock company based on the principles of European socialism. They divided the newspaper's stock into one hundred equal shares to allow employees to become owners.

During the 1840s, the *Tribune* was four pages long (that is, a single sheet of paper folded over). Reflecting the current popularity of the penny press, the paper contained articles on crime, scandal, and seductions drawn from the pens of its law reporter and police court reporter. The newspaper also covered such topics as agriculture, science, literature, and European thought. In these early years, Greeley himself wrote about three columns per day. The newspaper even served a social function in New York City, providing the opportunity for the "middle-aged gentleman" to open a correspondence with "a young lady" (addresses were kept confidential). By 1854, one issue of the *Tribune* contained 641 separate pieces, 510 of which were advertisements. Reading matter took about half the space. Five columns were devoted to "telegraphic intelligence" from across the country and the world.

During his tenure as *Tribune* editor, Greeley assembled an editorial staff of unusual talent and prominence. The list of nineteenth-century journalistic figures associated with the *Tribune* is impressive. Greeley's first assistant editor was Henry J. Raymond. While still a college student, Raymond contributed literary pieces to Greeley's *New-Yorker*. Greeley would later state that "a cleverer, readier, more generally efficient journalist, I never saw." In 1851, Raymond, with the support of Whig businessmen, left the *Tribune* to found the more conservative *New York Times*. One of Greeley's Washington correspondents during the 1850s was James Shepard Pike, who would later write an infamous indictment of "Negro rule" in South Carolina during Reconstruction, *The Prostate State* (1873). Henry C. Carey, the leading Republican economist, often wrote for Greeley's newspaper. Charles A. Dana became managing editor of the *Tribune* in 1849 after returning from Europe, where he had witnessed the European revolutions of 1848. Dana would most often manage the newspaper in Greeley's absence.

Perhaps Dana's most significant contribution to the *Tribune* was to hire the young German journalist and budding philosopher Karl Marx. The future founder of Communism began to write journalistically in the 1840s for the *Rheinische Zeitung* in Cologne and his own *Neue Rheinische Zeitung* founded in 1848 (the same year in which he published *The Manifesto of the Communist Party*). Marx, living in exile in England when he wrote to Dana in 1851, needed money, and the *Tribune* wanted correspondents to cover the revolutions of 1848. For the next nine years, Marx sent Greeley and Dana about two articles per week. These covered a wide range of topics, including British elections, revolutionary developments in Spain, and the role of China in world trade. Marx maintained an uneasy and somewhat ambivalent relationship with the *Tribune*. On the one hand, he did not think his articles represented his best work and often grew impatient with the editing the paper gave them. For their part, Dana and Greeley were not always sympathetic to the views of the German socialist. The editors once introduced a piece by disclaiming that "Mr. Marx has very decided opinions of his own, with some of which we are far from agreeing." In 1862, Dana ended the relationship.

The *Tribune* also brought within its orbit some of the finest writers in nineteenth-century American literature. George Ripley, the Transcendentalist founder of the utopian community experiment at Brook Farm, was at one time its book review editor. Essayist and future Mugwump intellectual George William Curtis also wrote for the *Tribune*.

Greeley nurtured literature in other ways as well. He negotiated with Nathaniel Hawthorne and Charles Dickens to publish their original works. He also served as the literary agent in New York for Henry David Thoreau. Greeley published Thoreau's essay "The Succession of Forest Trees" in the *Tribune* after the two had discussed forestry at Greeley's house in Chappaqua, New York. The New York editor and the Concord Transcendentalist developed other bonds as well: Greeley invited Thoreau to tutor his children at his home.

Perhaps the most important intellectual associated with the *Tribune* was Transcendentalist Margaret Fuller. Born in Cambridgeport, Massachusetts, in 1810, Fuller was largely taught by

The farm in Chappaqua, New York, where Horace Greeley spent much of his time. (Courtesy of the Library of Congress)

her Harvard-educated congressman father. An eager and precocious student, Margaret soon formed friendships with New England intellectuals James Freeman Clarke and Frederick Henry Hedge and held female-dominated conversational circles in the Boston home of Elizabeth Peabody. Along with Ralph Waldo Emerson and George Ripley, Fuller edited the Transcendentalist journal *The Dial* between 1840 and 1842. She was probably best known for *Woman in the Nineteenth Century* (1845), her powerful vindication of feminism. Greeley once called the book "the ablest, bravest, broadest, assertion yet made of what are termed Woman's Rights."

Margaret Fuller came to New York and the *Tribune* through the solicitations of both Horace and Molly Greeley. He first learned of her through *The Dial*. Upon reviewing her 1844 novel *Summer on the Lakes*, Greeley called Fuller "one of the most original as well as intellectual of American Women." Molly had met Fuller while in Boston and suggested that she work for the *Tribune*. Greeley hired Fuller as book review editor at a salary of $500 per year. Her first article in the *Tribune*, which appeared on December 7, 1844, was a review of Emerson's essays. Altogether, Margaret Fuller worked for the *Tribune* for about twenty months, writing an average of three articles a week. There was tension between Fuller and Greeley, perhaps because of his often contentious personality as editor and her adjustment to newspaper writing. "She could write only when in the vein," Greeley recalled, "and this needed often to be waited for through several days, while the occasion sometimes required an immediate utterance."

During her time in New York, Fuller also lived in the Greeleys' home on the banks of the East River across from Blackwell's Island. She considered the quiet rural getaway "entirely charming." Yet the harmony of nature was not matched in the Greeley household. "Fortune seemed to delight in placing us two in relations of friendly antagonism," Greeley explained about Fuller, "or rather, to develop all possible contrasts in our ideas and social habits." Margaret was inclined toward luxury and good appearance, while Horace was more spartan in his tastes. She found it hard to put up with the Grahamite diet of the Greeleys; he made comments on her choices of food that she found offensive. More substantially, the two editors argued over women's rights.

Fuller also developed a close relationship with Molly Greeley, but the female friendship was strained as Molly became increasingly despondent during the 1840s. "Our friend Mrs. Greeley," Fuller wrote in 1845, "is more dejected than ever." Yet Horace claimed that Margaret was the only person he knew "whose influence upon her was not irritating." The saving grace in the Greeley home was actually the relationship that developed between Margaret and the Greeleys' young son Arthur. "He clings to my neck," Fuller wrote, "and says little assenting sounds to the poetic remarks, and looks straight in my eyes." Greeley recalled that Fuller was especially good with children, "for no one had ever a more perfect faculty for entering into their sports, their feelings, their enjoyment."

In 1846, Fuller left the Greeley home and New York to serve as a *Tribune* correspondent in Europe. She met and had a son with Marquis Angelo Ossoli, a follower of Italian revolutionary leader Giuseppe Mazzini, and married Ossoli the next year. The entire family died tragically when their ship returning from Europe wrecked off of Fire Island, New York. Despite their domestic and editorial difficulties, Greeley and Fuller maintained a relationship of mutual respect. He recognized in her an unusually gifted mind and a benevolent heart. She considered him "a man of genuine excellence, honorable, benevolent, of an uncorrupted position, and, in his way, of even great abilities."

III

In the antebellum world of print culture, the press and literature enjoyed a close relationship. Notable poets Walt Whitman and William Cullen Bryant spent a substantial portion of their careers as editors. Literary "culture wars" between Whigs and Democrats were often carried on through newspapers and periodicals. Greeley's first venture into independent journalism illustrates the connection among politics, literature, and newspapers.

The *New-Yorker* began publication in the spring of 1834 when Greeley was twenty-three years old. The first issue sold only a hundred copies, but by September, Greeley was selling roughly 2,500 copies. By 1837, the circulation was up to 9,500 copies, a larger figure than any other literary periodical at the time. The *New-Yorker* copiously republished literature, poetry, and essays from other writers in the United States and Europe. It included short sections on local and national news. Greeley included his own editorials on political and moral questions ranging from banks to European politics. Despite its increased popularity, the *New-Yorker* was always in financial straits. Greeley was not a great businessman and, like many Americans, suffered financially from the Panic of 1837. In 1838, subscribers owed him close to $8,000. Greeley was forced to cease publishing the newspaper in July 1841, but by then he was editing the *Tribune*.

Implicit in Greeley's approach to literature were Whiggish values of moral improvement rooted in a Unitarian literary aesthetic. According to its most astute student, "Literature was, for the Unitarian moral philosophers, an important means of social control as well as an invaluable aid to personality development. It helped form the taste, refine the sentiments, and determine the manners of a people." Unitarian thinkers believed that literary pursuits should have the goal of "improvement." They assumed that an elite intellectual class could and should pass aesthetic judgment. With these goals in mind, Boston Unitarians launched the *North American Review*, which served as the critical voice of New England Unitarianism. These philosopher-critics drew upon an aesthetic approach pioneered by Scottish moral philosophers Frances Hutcheson and Adam Smith, based on the assumption that art could stimulate the sentiments. Ideologically akin to New England Unitarianism, American Whig literary critics emphasized the importance of morality in literature. They believed that literature could reinforce values of balance, character, harmony, and paternalism: "Whig literary critics considered themselves not only arbiters of taste but shapers of manners and morals."

The literary reviews in the *New-Yorker* followed these precepts. A section titled "Domestic Literature" provided the readers of the *New-Yorker* with short reviews of publications. As Greeley explained in 1837, "Brief notices of new books, pamphlets, periodicals, and occasionally of the Drama and other sources of public amusement, will likewise be given." Greeley's reviews of books and magazines amounted to short lessons in moral instruction. The editor freely acknowledged that he could accomplish a useful purpose by "holding up to public fosterage, works describing praise, or pointing out the evils that may flow from the injudicious perusal of all the tomes belched from the prolific press." Historian Daniel Walker Howe has characterized Greeley as "an intensely didactic man." His literary reviews were part of his larger reform impulse, "the imposition of a new, more rational order."

Literary magazines were given prominent attention by the *New-Yorker*. One of the earliest and most important of these, the *American Monthly Magazine*, began publication in 1829. In the next decade, the *Knickerbocker* (1833) and the *Southern Literary Messenger* (1834) figured conspicuously in the pages of the *New-Yorker*. Beginning in 1837, Greeley spent more than an ordinary amount of time and space on the *United States Magazine and Democratic Review*. This journal was the literary expression of a movement within the Democratic Party known as Young America. As a Whig editor, Greeley contributed to the decade-long feud between literary critics of two opposing camps in New York, one centered around the *Knickerbocker* and the other centered around the literary nationalists of Young America.

In his first notice of the *Democratic Review*, Greeley warned that the journal "could not properly be regarded as a mere party advocate or organ" if it truly wanted to be a literary magazine. Reflecting the strain of anti-partyism in nineteenth-century American political culture, Greeley believed that a truly literary magazine could offset the dangerous tendencies of parties to forget their pledges and principles. He thus warned the editors of the *Democratic Review* that they "must not overlay their literature with too much of politics." In a similar vein, Greeley noted that *The Reformer*, a journal edited by Richmond *Whig* editor Richard K. Cralle, was conducted "with an intensity of Opposition spirit bordering on ferocity."

Greeley also reviewed fiction, which one cultural historian has termed "the most striking development in American literature

after 1820." Some familiar names in the canon of the American
Renaissance appeared in the pages of the *New-Yorker*. In 1838,
Greeley noted the publication of Nathaniel Hawthorne's *Tales
of the Province House*, which in his opinion "could not fail to be
interesting." The novels of Maria Edgeworth received appreciative
reviews. British and American readers in the early nineteenth century, along with Unitarian critics such as Andrews Norton and Levi
Frisbee, greatly admired Edgeworth. Greeley claimed similarly that
young readers have "stored their memories with the rich moralities
that characterize all her productions, and breathe through every
passage of these practical and simple stories." American novelist
James Kirke Paulding was not as fortunate as Edgeworth. In one
short notice of his novels, Greeley admitted that "we have never
regarded Mr. Paulding as gifted with the highest order of creative
talent."

The *New-Yorker* regularly reviewed Greek and Roman literature
published by the Harper's Classical Library as well. Even though
Greeley believed that the classics should be made widely available
and often lauded their style, he failed to appreciate their value. For instance, he claimed that Livy was "not the most profound of historians,
[and] neither are his statements uniformly to be relied on." Greeley
was equally critical of Homer (translated by Alexander Pope). Even
though he acknowledged that Homer's epic poems were "of the highest effort of the human intellect among a rude and barbarous people,"
he insisted that it was "inferior in character and effort" to modern
poetic efforts that were more "philosophic and intellectual." A similar
critical fate befell Horace, whom Greeley considered an "offender
against the canons of moral purity both in sentiment and diction."

Whether reviewing literary magazines, fiction, or the classics,
Greeley followed the aesthetic principle that literature should have
moral purpose. Unitarian scholar Andrews Norton claimed that "a
large portion of the most effective precepts and exhortations that
have been addressed to men have been conveyed to them in some
sort of fiction." Greeley made his own critical standards explicit
in an editorial on May 19, 1838: "When we observe or fancy the
existence of dangerous moral obliquity in volumes submitted to us

for criticism, we feel constrained to notice the fact, however reluctantly." In Greeley's view, style was related to content. To be didactic, good literature had first to be clearly understood. "If poetry, to be correct, should be graded to a level with the comprehension of the uneducated mass," Greeley noted, "then we think the poem of which we are now discoursing possesses merit, as it is clear of unnecessary verbiage, and attempts no flights into realms where common sense refuses to follow." Greeley wrote similarly in a review of a novel by Grace Kennedy: "The style is remarkably plain and unaffected, and the moral does not require a microscope for its discovery, as the moral of modern stories too often does." Greeley was clearly critical of what he described as "the exaggerated sentiment, inflated style, and pompous diction of too large a portion of the literature of the day."

Contemporary French literature was a specific target of Greeley's criticism. He praised an article on French novels and novelists published in the *London Quarterly Review* as "a most powerful and salutary exhibition of the immorality, the blasphemy, the gross indecency and inconceivable abominations of Parisian romance." Greeley considered the modern French novel "a most pernicious school." He clearly saw in French literature the subversive specter of the French Revolution. "The world knows well, that the daring speculations of the Atheistic philosophers and the licentious romances of Crebillion and his compatriots in evil did much to overturn the social fabric of France and produce the horrors of the Revolution."

IV

As the *New-Yorker* gave way to the *Tribune* in 1841, Greeley had proven his abilities as a newspaper editor. In the coming decade, he would continue to push for Whig economic and moral reform. He would grow increasingly wary of and vocal about slaveholding expansion. He would also pursue a variety of more radical reforms that questioned the social and economic order of late Jacksonian America.

Chapter Four

═══════════════○═══════════════

The Politics of Reform
The 1840s

LOOKING BACK ON HIS PUBLIC LIFE, Horace Greeley recalled that in "modern society, all things tend unconsciously toward grand, comprehensive, pervading reforms." The spirit of liberal reform abounded in the United States during the 1840s. "We are to revise the whole of our structure," Transcendentalist Ralph Waldo Emerson proclaimed in 1841, "the state, the school, religion, marriage, trade, science and explore their foundation in our nature." Inspired by a democratic impulse and the missionary zeal of the Second Great Awakening, Americans embraced a myriad of organized and individual efforts to reform their society. They attacked such contemporary evils as slavery, drinking, and war, while building new prisons and mental hospitals. A few sought to create a utopian society through communities like Brook Farm, Amana, Zoar, and New Harmony. Emerson's protégé, Henry David Thoreau, even created his own personal utopia at Walden Pond in Massachusetts. From 1845 to 1847, Thoreau built a cabin in the woods "to live deliberately, to front only the essential facts of life, and see if I could not learn what it had to teach, and not, when I came to die, discover that I had not lived."

Along with his role as newspaper editor, Whig politician, and antislavery Republican, Greeley rightly enjoys a reputation as a reformer. He was an early convert to temperance, perhaps the most widespread of these movements. Probably in response to his father's heavy drinking, Greeley made an open pledge of his temperance in 1824 in Westhaven, Vermont. He helped establish the first temperance club in East Poultney, Vermont. In the 1850s, Greeley supported the so-called Maine Law, which prohibited the manufacturing and sale of intoxicating beverages.

Temperance was only the beginning for Greeley, however. In 1838, he spent one Sunday with the Shakers. He attended a peace conference in London and openly gave voice to women's rights. When women were denied representation at a world temperance convention, Greeley sarcastically suggested that they call it "An Orthodox White Male Adult Saints' Convention." He lived in a New York boardinghouse run on the dietary principles of Sylvester Graham. Greeley took the Fox sisters, spiritualists Maggie and Katie, into his home, claiming that "it would be the basest cowardice not to say that we are convinced beyond a doubt of their perfect integrity and good faith" (though Greeley later claimed that he felt the rappings were a fraud).

Greeley thus touched most of the currents of reform that were running through American society in the three decades before the Civil War. The Northern assault on slavery, perhaps the most momentous challenge of reformers to the structure of American life, would occupy him more fully during the 1850s. During the 1840s, Greeley's reform efforts focused in one way or another on land and labor. He became one of America's leading Associationists, a group of people who attempted to build a new social and economic landscape on the ideas of French reformer Charles Fourier. Greeley was also an enthusiastic proponent of land reform through the National Reform Association. Finally, his recognition of the centrality of landownership to freedom and citizenship drew his attention to two populist impulses of the 1840s, the Anti-Rent War in New York and the Dorr Rebellion in Rhode Island. Greeley's attitudes toward these reform crusades of the 1840s reveal the possibilities and limitations of Whig middle-class liberalism when confronted with the capitalist transformation of late Jacksonian America.

I

Greeley's attraction to Associationism was rooted in the social and economic dislocations that accompanied America's transition to capitalism. As the Panic of 1837 headed into its first winter, Greeley warned that at least ten thousand New Yorkers were "in utter and hopeless distress" and might not survive the winter. Between 1837 and 1838, the number of New Yorkers seeking relief rose from under thirty thousand to more than eighty thousand. In 1838, "times were so hard," noted an alarmed editor of the *Sunday Morning Atlas*, that unemployed women had been driven to selling cigars! The depression even affected New York's theater business. Hard times forced theater managers to become more innovative and spectacular in wooing customers. In presenting the drama *The Pirate's Signal* at New York's Bowery Theatre, for example, one manager replaced the stage with a large tank of water on which a full-rigged ship floated with actors.

As part of a committee for relief in New York's Sixth Ward, Greeley witnessed firsthand the suffering from the depression. His confrontation with the damages of early industrial capitalism shaped his approach to political economy. Already deeply imbued with the values of Whiggery, Greeley clung firmly to the value of free-market capitalism. He lamented inefficiency in production and consumption. He could not see why there should be any paupers except those who were disabled. "Where labor stands idle, save in the presence of some great public calamity," Greeley stated, "there is a demonstrated deficiency, not of Capital, but of brains." Such thinking led him to an enthusiastic embrace of planned social and economic communities as an antidote to the perils of capitalism.

"I believe in Association, or Cooperation, or whatever name may be given to the combination of many heads and hands to achieve a beneficent result, which is beyond the means of one or a few of them," Greeley wrote in his *Recollections*, "for I perceive that vast economies, and vastly increased efficiency, may thus be secured." The economic advantages were clear: "It shall yet be

proved that the combined efforts of many workers make Labor efficient and ennobling, as well as attractive." Greeley once calculated
that combination "ought to add twenty-five per cent to the average
income of the thriftier half of the laboring class."

The philosophy of Association rested upon a belief in the essential sociability of human beings. Greeley maintained that "man's
intellectual and inventive faculties [are] stimulated by contact with
his fellow-men." In the 1840s, Greeley's chosen form of commu-
nitarianism was Fourierism. In a letter to Emerson, Greeley wrote
that Fourier's form of Association was "the most natural thing in the
world for a properly civilized and Christianized society—the very best
to which all the Progress of the last century has tended by a natural
law." As editor of the influential *Tribune*, Greeley became instrumental in the spread of Fourierite socialism in antebellum America.

Charles Fourier (1772–1837) was a French mathematician and
social thinker—according to Greeley, "a poor clerk, reserved and
taciturn, whose hard, dogmatic, algebraic style seemed expressly
calculated to discourage readers and repel adherents; so that his
disciples were few indeed, down to the date of his death in 1837."
Fourier devised a rather complicated and rigid plan to reorganize
society in small units called *phalanxes*. Each phalanx would consist
of 1,620 people, including laborers, capitalists, and men of talent.
They would represent two of each "passional type" of human being.
To maintain harmony, Fourier would exclude soldiers, philosophers, political economists, and lawyers. Each phalanx would function as a joint stock company, with every member receiving equal
portions of the common product. The remainder would be divided
in twelfths: five to labor, four to capital, and three to talent. Phalanxes would be constructed with common living and dining areas.

In November 1841, Greeley summarized his understanding of
Fourierism as "a system of Industrial and Household Association,
on the principle of Joint Stock Investment, whereby Labor will be
ennobled and rendered attractive and universal, Capital be offered
a secure and lucrative investment, and Talent and Industry find
appropriate, constant employment, and adequate reward, while
Plenty, comfort, and the best means of Intellectual and Moral Improvement is guaranteed to all, regardless of former acquirements

or condition." He quickly became an enthusiastic convert to Fourierism, confidently stating in 1842 that the French social philosopher had, "by a patient study of Human Nature and its tendencies, discovered that Social Order, the same as a man might discover the plan of a machine by examining carefully the springs and wheels belonging to it."

Albert Brisbane served as the major popularizer of Fourier's ideas in the United States during the 1840s. In fact, it was Brisbane who renamed Fourierism "Association" for his more pragmatic American audience. Born in New York in 1809, Brisbane was the child of an English father and Scottish mother. Greeley recalled him as "a young man of liberal education and varied culture." Brisbane had traveled in Europe, where he encountered the French socialists Fourier and Claude Henri de Saint-Simon. He articulated Fourier's ideas in a book titled *The Social Destiny of Man; or, Association and Reorganization of Industry* (1840). "Albert Brisbane brought the message," James Parton recalled. "Horace Greeley heard and believed it."

On October 21, 1841, Greeley published a notice of Brisbane's lectures that caught their essential message: "a system of Association, or the binding up of individual and family interests in Social and Industrial Communities, wherein all faculties may be developed, all energies usefully employed, all legitimate desires satisfied, and idleness, want, temptation and crime be annihilated. In such Association, individual property will be maintained, the family be held sacred, and every inducement held out to a proper ambition." In 1842, a group of Fourierites purchased a column in the *Tribune* that originally ran daily, and later three times a week, until 1844.

Associationism continued throughout the 1840s to be an important element in Greeley's journalism. In late 1846 and 1847, he debated its merits with Henry J. Raymond of the New York *Courier & Enquirer*. Raymond had previously worked with the *Tribune* before joining James Watson Webb at the *Courier & Enquirer*. A more traditional Whig, Raymond was determined to expose Greeley's inordinate attention to reform measures by attacking him as a socialist. Greeley and Raymond agreed to pen twelve articles debating Fourier's system in each paper.

Greeley began his "Association Discussed, No. 1" with propo-
sitions "intended to show that Justice to the Poor and Wretched
demands of the more fortunate classes a radical Social Reform."
Men possessed the natural right to earn a living from the soil, yet
Americans of Greeley's day had not followed "Nature's rule of allowing no man to appropriate to himself any more of the earth than
he can cultivate." The result was a concentration of landownership
in a few hands, as was especially evident in the Hudson River Valley of New York. Consequently, "as Population increases and Arts
are perfected, the income of the wealthy owner of land increases
while the recompense of the hired or leasehold cultivator is steadily
diminishing." Greeley's primary justification for Associationism
would become the basis for his involvement in land reform: "THE
RIGHT TO LABOR, secured to them in the creation of the earth,
taken away in the granting of the Soil to a minor portion of them,
must be restored." This could only be achieved, he argued, by "a
radical change in our Social Economy." The advantages of Association would be in the economy of land, fuel, labor, and "in Imple-
ments of Culture and Industry generally."

The debate with Raymond lasted six months. "It was conducted
on both sides," Parton recalled, "with spirit and ability, and it attracted much attention." The exchange provided Greeley with an
opportunity to define and defend Fourierite principles.

Greeley's involvement in Associationism went beyond editing
and writing. He joined a church founded by William Henry Channing in New York in 1843, called the Christian Union, and became
president of the American Union of Associationists in 1850, after
the movement was beginning to decline. Convinced that the phalanx was a cooperative "republican organization," Greeley became
involved in the Grand Prairie Harmonial Institute in Indiana and
Nauvoo, Illinois. He attended Fourierite conventions that met in
Rochester, New York, in 1843 and Boston in 1844.

Greeley was involved with two Fourierite communities in particular. Sylvania Phalanx, in Pike County, Pennsylvania, consisted
of three thousand acres of land along the Delaware River. Founded
in 1843 with twenty-eight couples, its purpose, according to Greeley, was to establish a "new, more trustful, more benignant relation-

ship between Capital and Labor." It consisted of three two-story houses, a gristmill, a sawmill, and a store. Greeley himself helped finance the project, hoping it would prove "the feasibility and the signal advantages of Industrial Association." He served as treasurer of the phalanx and visited the community, where he contributed his labor to farming. The Fourierite experiment at Sylvania dissolved in 1845 after a harsh winter destroyed most of the crops. In 1892, the remainder of the town was renamed Greeley in tribute to his support.

The other community that was of particular interest to Greeley was the North American Phalanx, a 673-acre farm on Colt's Neck in New Jersey. He contributed to the initial capital, owned the largest number of shares, and served as its vice president. "Here we few, but zealous Associationists of New York and its vicinity for a time concentrated our means and our efforts," Greeley later recalled. Besides producing wheat, flour, and other crops, the North American Phalanx sold the first boxed cereal in the United States. In 1849, the land and buildings were assessed at more than $50,000. A fire in 1854, though, destroyed many of its buildings. "Its means had been larger," Greeley remembered, "its men and

Attack on Greeley (far right) as a free-soil and Fourierite reformer. (Courtesy of the Library of Congress)

women, in the average, more capable and devoted, than those of any rival; if it could not live, there was no hope for any of them."

Greeley's embrace of Fourierite Associationism provoked criticism. He recalled that the public at the time regarded socialistic schemes with "stubborn indifference." His support of this kind of communitarian reform drew opposition from fellow editors at the New York *Express* and Rochester *Evening Post*. Universalist leader Hosea Ballou criticized Fourierists as utopian dreamers. Even fellow New York Whig Thurlow Weed opposed Greeley's socialist ideas, which led to some conflict between the two. "Do not assume to dictate or lecture me," Greeley pointedly once told Weed.

Horace Greeley's advocacy of Associationism is important for several reasons. For one, it rehearsed ideas that would appear elsewhere, specifically in land reform. It also laid bare his fundamental affirmation of the basic tenets of liberal capitalism, reflecting Greeley's persistent emphasis on the essential harmony between classes. Finally, it confirmed his commitment to private property as the basis of economic society: "The natural right to Individual Property has its origin in Labor. He who cuts a tree in the forest and fashions it into a canoe or a cradle, has an exclusive right to the article he has thus made provided he has left timber to others wherefrom to make themselves canoes or cradles."

Greeley's most recent biographer calls Associationism "a kind of utopian middle-class capitalism, where laborers could become property owners, and where hard work would lead to individual rewards and civic virtue." Greeley often took pains to dissociate Associationism from the more radical ideas of Robert Owen and Fanny Wright, once stating that "a complete and radical difference exists between their social views and the Social System which we advocate." Accordingly, Greeley denied that Association meant communism. Indeed, he considered communism at war with "one of the strongest and most universal instincts,—that which impels each worker to produce and save for himself and his own." Greeley agreed with Fourier that "Communism must destroy individual liberty."

II

During the 1840s, Greeley eagerly joined the movement for land reform. In a *Tribune* editorial of July 15, 1842, Greeley suggested another cure for the vicissitudes of a market economy: "There are thousands of Laboring Men now in our City—many of them with wives and children—who are hanging on from week to week with nothing to do—hoping and perhaps seeking work, but obtaining little or none. Once for all, we beg and entreat them to GO INTO THE COUNTRY—Go now, at once, without hesitation or delay."

Antebellum American land reform was aimed at increasing opportunities for individual landownership, especially in low-priced public lands in the West. It was a capitalist solution to problems created by capitalism. Land reform drew upon the long association in Anglo-American thought between land and freedom, and the natural-law argument that each man had a right to land. John Locke, for example, had predicated his political theories on the idea of land as property. Thomas Paine, in such works as *Agrarian Justice*, linked landownership to citizenship. In the early nineteenth century, Jeffersonians had extolled farming as an incubator of republican virtue. Greeley's views on land were shaped as well by Thomas Carlyle's *Past and Present*, a copy of which he received from Emerson. Greeley called it a "great book—a noble book." So enthralled was the New York editor that he urged a friend to read it and told him he would go without sleep in order to give it more readings.

During the 1830s, Jacksonian Democratic radicals in eastern cities gave land reform an important impetus. It was a popular subject among leaders of the emerging workingmen's movement, which was responding to the threats the new system of factory production posed to the artisan republican tradition of equal rights and independence. Thomas Skidmore, in *The Rights of Man to Property!* (1829), called for government enforcement of equality of property. Active in the workingmen's movement in New York, Skidmore helped introduce the concept that land reform might be one potential solution to the problems of the workingman. The land reformers thus garnered support from alienated urban artisans such as shoe workers in factory towns like Lynn, Massachusetts.

George Henry Evans was the leader of the land reform movement in antebellum America. Born in Britain, Evans became the editor of the *Radical* and the *Working Man's Advocate*. He urged that free land be made available from the public domain for all Americans. He wanted to give this land to settlers rather than speculators, prohibit its alienation, and break up large landed estates. In March 1844, Evans organized the National Reform Association based on a program of federal homestead legislation, homestead exemption for those suffering from debt, and limits on land allotments to prevent speculation. Greeley considered the principles of the National Reform Association "the best that can be devised."

Greeley was particularly active in land reform between 1845 and 1848. He attended a convention of land reformers in New York in October 1845 and gave a speech before the New York Young Men's National Reform Association. Greeley shared the agrarian emphasis of the land reformers, foreshadowing the link between land and freedom embodied in the ideology of the free soil movement. "Wherever the ownership of the soil is so engrossed by a small part of the community," he explained, "that the far larger number are compelled to pay whatever the few may see fit to exact for the privilege of occupying and cultivating the earth, there is something like slavery." Greeley worked through the political system to advance the cause of land reform. He supported a state constitutional limit on individual landholdings in the mid-1840s. In his short stint in Congress during the 1850s, Greeley would introduce a bill "authorizing each landless citizen of the United States to occupy and appropriate a small allotment of the National Domain free of charge."

Greeley remains well known for popularizing, through the *Tribune*, the "safety-valve" explanation for land reform. Free homesteads would provide a solution for urban overcrowding and poverty. "The freedom of public lands to actual settlers," he explained in 1846, "and the limitation of future acquisition of land to some reasonable amount, are also measures which seem to us vitally necessary to the ultimate emancipation of labor from thralldom and misery." Abundant land would provide a place for excess workers, consequently raising wages in eastern cities. Greeley argued that the city was "a hard place for a destitute man"; in the country, on the other hand, "he who is temperate, industrious and upright is never in danger of enforced idleness or of absolute want; and if he gains no property, he is constantly gaining character and standing which answers the same purpose with many better ones." The granting of individual homesteads would thus assure that "every man may at least eat the bread of Industry and Independence." Greeley's arguments for land reform embodied a vision of a harmonious middle-class agrarian order: "A primary object with a man who emigrates should be to pitch his tent where are the benefits of society, school, mills, roads, in connexion with cheap lands, good markets for produce and a steady demand for labor."

A close bond existed in the 1840s between land reformers and Associationists, as both groups shared the assumption that a change in environment could improve human character. The *Harbinger*, the official journal of American Associationists, affirmed that "this movement is far deeper than any that has ever before been undertaken by the Working Classes, and it is a gratifying sign of the increase of intelligence among them with regard to the importance of true and organic reform." Besides Greeley, Parke Godwin, William Henry Channing, and Albert Brisbane were followers of both Charles Fourier and George Henry Evans. In both movements, Greeley pushed the boundaries of Whiggish liberalism to endorse more radical social experiments. In fact, he adhered to the producerist, labor theory of value that was at the core of the values of Jacksonian workingmen. Yet at the same time Greeley remained committed to the private ownership of property, a pillar of capitalist political economy.

III

The link between land and democracy was also manifested in what has become known as the New York Anti-Rent War. This conflict, which at times escalated into open violence, pitted tenant farmers against large and powerful landlords in the Hudson River Valley. Protesters wanted to tear down what they saw as an antiquated and oppressive system of leasehold estates in upstate New York and distribute land to farmers as independent freeholds. As a vivid expression of democratic dissent in antebellum America, the Anti-Rent War involved between twenty-five thousand and sixty thousand supporters in eleven counties. As a newspaper editor, New York Whig, and reformer, Horace Greeley was drawn into the vortex of this conflict. For Greeley, as for other Americans, anti-rent protests brought to the surface the tension between property rights and land distribution—essentially, between capitalism and democracy. On the one hand, Greeley sympathized with the tenant farmers due to his belief that individual freeholds provided the basis for freedom. Yet his adherence to his basic principles of property ownership and social order distanced him from the more radical, extralegal means of anti-rent protest.

The roots of the New York anti-rent movement lay in the state's colonial past. In the early seventeenth century, the Dutch had granted large tracts of land, called *patroonships*, to selected settlers in the Hudson and Mohawk Valleys. They were large-scale private agricultural estates resembling European manorial estates. "The charter from Queen Anne is baronial or feudal, conferring upon the Patroon all the rights of a lord of the manor under the old English laws," Greeley explained. For example, the patroon could hold courts, issue writs, and impose fines. The renters of land were obligated to pay rent in kind or money and to provide a day's service with a team or carriage, and they were subject to limitations on mining and water privileges. Paradoxically, this aristocratic system of landowners and leaseholds survived the Revolution. One of the largest patroonships was the manor of Rensselaerswyck, which consisted of roughly 750,000 acres on both sides of the Hudson River. Livingston Manor in Columbia County was another patroonship that figured largely in the Anti-Rent War. The landlords of these and other manors remained strong in the New York Constitutional Convention of 1821 where leading families like the Livingstons and Van Rensselaers and their allies opposed universal manhood suffrage.

While conflicts between landholders and tenant farmers had occurred in the mid-eighteenth century, a series of social and economic changes in the early nineteenth century triggered another agrarian class confrontation. The Holland Land Company purchased lands west of the Genesee River and sold it to wealthy landlords. However, the New England farmers who moved into western New York looking for land wanted freeholds or the opportunity to own their own land.

Along with this growing population, deforestation, the transition from grain cultivation to livestock, and increasing access to markets via the Erie Canal created other conditions for conflict. Stephen Van Rensselaer and Robert L. Livingston made greater efforts to collect rents, leading to more suits during the 1820s. A stalwart Federalist, Van Rensselaer was considered a kind of benevolent paternalist. After his death in 1839, Greeley described him as "a very kind-hearted, benevolent man, and popular with his tenantry." Van Rensselaer's two sons, unlike their father, pressed harder for rent payments and the fulfillment of contracts. Tenant farmers resisted these efforts at greater control of their property and fought for the benefits of improvement they had provided to the land. Anti-renters claimed that tenancy discouraged improvement and "successful husbandry."

Anti-rent agitation spread throughout upstate New York in 1844 and 1845. Protesting farmers at first drew upon the means of popular politics that had been developed through the anti-Masonic movement and the rise of the two-party system. They led rent boycotts and organized town, county, and state committees. Thousands of anti-renters joined associations in the summer of 1844. Anti-rent state conventions were held in January 1845 and February 1846. Leaders published newspapers like the Albany *Freeholder* and Thomas Devyr's *Anti-Renter*. George Henry Evans and the National Reformers offered their support at their national convention in the summer of 1846. Devyr, in fact, was also active in the land reform movement.

Anti-renters based their arguments on the fundamental principle of equal rights, along with more specific legal arguments on the defectiveness of some of the land titles. A number of anti-renters had already drawn upon more aggressive forms of agrarian protest reminiscent of Shays's Rebellion. These tenants organized secret groups known as "Indians," filled with young men and the landless or land-poor, who intimidated landlords and their agents and met efforts toward law enforcement with violence.

By the mid-1840s, anti-renters also pursued their cause through electoral politics. They nominated their own candidates for the state legislature and supported candidates for local elections in Rensselaer, Schoharie, and other counties. Liberal Whig Ira Harris was one of these anti-rent candidates, which Greeley considered "an act of the most amazing stupidity," fearing it would alienate the conservatives in the Whig Party. The anti-renters' political strategy was aimed at forcing Whigs and Democrats to bid for their support.

The liberal, or progressive, wing of the Whig Party in New York took up the cause of the anti-renters. Governor William Henry Seward disliked the leasehold system and in 1840 urged the state legislature to consider remedial legislation. Whigs saw the old leaseholds as an outdated impediment, not unlike slavery, to their visions of improvement. Not surprisingly, liberal Whigs wanted reform through legislative and constitutional means. Although they were alarmed by the violence that was occurring, they still opposed the use of force.

Greeley's reaction to the New York anti-rent movement reflected his ambivalence toward democratic reform in the 1840s. On the one hand, he supported the cause of the tenants. Acknowledging the rights of private property, Greeley nonetheless maintained "that there are other rights also precious, also venerable, also demanding deference—namely, the Rights of Man. The Right of Man to live, and of course to an opportunity to procure a subsistence, will one of these days demand consideration." Even as he called for the suppression of violence, Greeley thought that "public attention should be called to the grievances of the tenants, which are most serious, and in our judgment, *must* be removed." Greeley shared the Whigs' belief that the leasehold system was an anachronism, standing in the way of progress. Feudal elements from the original grant, he explained, "are still more objectionable, because directly calculated to arrest and discourage improvement." Under the current conditions, renters could not profit from improvements they made. Ever seeking harmony between capital and labor, Greeley urged that the patroons "come forward and make a magnanimous offer of compromise with the tenants for the extinction of the feudal tenure."

On the other hand, Greeley recognized the rights of property owners involved in the conflict. He claimed that the proprietor was still entitled to rent and services. Indeed, the patroon's conditions "do not appear to us as unreasonable." Greeley even acknowledged a place for a paternalistic capitalism. "We think the true relation between a Patroon and his tenantry," he explained, "is more patriarchal, more intimate and kindly, than that which properly exists between the owner of a block of houses and his tenants." Greeley tended to see the problem as a breakdown in what should have been a harmonious relationship. The landlord's indifference and isolation had led to the discontent of the renters. The patroon should never have employed lawyers. Rather, "Christianity and a true Humanity counsel an entirely different course." Above all, Greeley deplored the recourse to violent, extraconstitutional means of protest: "From the first to last we have urged that all these 'Indian' operations should be put down with a strong hand—that, no matter how real are the grievances of the tenants or how righteous their demands, any organized resistance or obstruction to the administration of the laws is a flagrant crime, to be sternly repressed and punished."

Like other liberal Whigs, Horace Greeley began to see in the late 1840s that movements like the New York anti-renters could unite with opponents of slavery in an anti-aristocratic free soil crusade. Yet before that could happen, Greeley was drawn to another democratic insurgency, this time emanating from Rhode Island.

IV

Like the Anti-Rent War, the Dorr Rebellion in Rhode Island was a significant episode in the struggle over democratization in the United States before the Civil War. "In no other state," explains historian Sean Wilentz, "did a landed elite square off so sharply or so violently against a growing manufacturing working class and its liberal sympathizers."

As in New York, the source of conflict lay in the colonial past. The old colonial charter of Rhode Island had been liberal in its time, with a property qualification for voting of only $134 in land value or $7 in rent. "It was framed for an infant community," Greeley observed, "wholly agricultural, with land cheap and abundant all around them; and in point of fact almost every adult male was a landholder." He called it "a most liberal and excellent one for the time, but rather out of date now." Greeley was right, for the colonial charter essentially disfranchised about 50 percent of potential voters by 1840.

Demands for reform followed Rhode Island's shift from an agrarian to an industrialized state. "The transition from an Agricultural to a Manufacturing community," Greeley maintained, "has developed and aggravated the theoretical defects of the Rhode Island frame of Government." Protest emerged from industrial towns such as Providence and Pawtucket with rising numbers of immigrants and wage laborers. Greeley articulated their cause: "Not one-third of the Citizens of Rhode Island are now Landholders, or engaged in Agriculture at all; and it is not too much to say that a full half of the intelligence, political capacity and moral worth are possessed by those who own no soil."

As its name suggests, the Dorr Rebellion owed much of its force and direction to a powerful leader named Dorr. Thomas Wilson Dorr, the son of a wealthy Providence Federalist, was born in 1805. He studied at Exeter Academy and Harvard University before studying law with conservative New York jurist James Kent, who, as it happens, had opposed the broadening of suffrage at New York's constitutional convention in 1821. Dorr became a critic of suffrage restrictions in Rhode Island and therefore left his state's

Whig Party. In 1832, he confessed that he had not "yet lived to a purpose." That design would not be long in coming.

Protest against suffrage restrictions by non-landholders appeared after the presidential election of 1832. The workingmen's parties were the first group to speak out. Seth Luther, in his *Address on the Right of Free Suffrage* (1832), insisted on political equality for workingmen. Next was a group of moderate reformers and Whigs, including the influential Dorr, who founded the Rhode Island Constitutional Party in 1833. They pushed for a constitutional convention but were unable to convince the sitting legislature. In 1837, this group formed the Democratic Constitutionalist Party. In the spring of 1840, a Rhode Island Suffrage Association was established with support from working-class leaders like Luther.

By the early 1840s, the Dorrite movement was beginning to take shape as protesters began to consider more radical, extralegal measures. Ignoring the existing legislature, in October 1841 they proclaimed their own "People's Constitution," which included calls for universal male suffrage and an independent judiciary. Sensing the tremors of protest, state government officeholders called for a constitutional convention, which wrote a new constitution bowing to popular rule. However, it was rejected in a referendum by voters in town meetings. In the spring of 1842, Dorr and his followers began to set up their own government, swearing in officials and establishing committees. As Greeley summarized the situation in 1842, "Thus the government party were thrown back upon the old Charter, in defiance of their wish and their effort to concede a more liberal suffrage; while the 'Suffrage' party contended that *their* Constitution had been legally adopted and was now the paramount law of the State." The governor struck back and began arresting Dorrite leaders for treason under what were called "Algernine" laws. President John Tyler, facing pressure from both sides, sought some kind of conciliation, but to no avail. In March 1842, Greeley worried that a "fearful crisis now impends."

On the moonless, foggy night of May 17–18, 1842, the Dorr Rebellion broke out. Dorrite forces attempted to seize the state arsenal in Providence by force. They were backed by workingmen, including Luther and working-class hero Mike Walsh, who

had promised to lay waste to the city of Providence. Dorr's followers also had the promise of aid from local militia companies.
But the rebellion moved rapidly toward a tragicomic ending. In
a show of strength by the Law and Order Party, the Providence
arsenal was heavily defended by the government. After their can-
non misfired, Dorr's disorganized forces withdrew. Dorr himself
fled, while many of his supporters, Luther among them, were
arrested.

Partisan politics soon entered the Dorrite fray as it had during the Anti-Rent War in New York. Many Democrats saw this
as a contest between aristocracy and democracy and sympathized
with the Dorrites. Martin Van Buren expressed his "most hearty
sympathy" for the Dorrites. New York Democrats William Cullen
Bryant and Churchill C. Cambreleng, as well as working-class
radicals Alexander Ming and Levi D. Slamm, voiced their support
for the Dorrite cause. Ely Moore, first president of the General
Trades' Union, wrote a letter that was read at a meeting of New
York Tammany Hall Democrats in April 1842 in support of the
Dorrites.

"Dorr was but the deluded and maddened instrument," Greeley
complained, "of the desperate demagogues of our City—of Purdy,
D'Avozac, Vanderpoel, Slamm, Cambreleng and Company." Greeley considered the Dorr revolt a pretext for the Democrats of Tammany Hall to attack President Tyler. He insisted that "the guilt and
condemnation will rest heavily on *their* souls who at this distance
have recklessly stirred up the fires of a wholly needless sedition and
warfare to subserve their own party advantage and sordid lust of
power." As late as 1844, Greeley was still complaining that "Loco-
Foco journals are hard at work on endeavors to excite sympathy for
Thomas W. Dorr."

The more conservative Whig Party was horrified at this assault
upon existing political institutions. The Hartford *Courant*, for instance, compared the Dorrites to "the Fanny Wrights, Robert Dale
Owens, O.A. Brownson, and their fellow laborers against the social
system of our country." Governor Seward considered the Dorr Rebellion treason.

As he had in the Anti-Rent War, Greeley demonstrated ambivalence toward the Dorrites. Once again, he sympathized with the goals of the suffrage reformers and hoped that "the Freeholders will see the propriety of conceding to the just demands of their brethren and extension of the Right of Suffrage." The disfranchised voters of Rhode Island, he said, "have long enough appealed in vain for redress." Yet, in general, Greeley was seriously concerned with the implications of the Dorr Rebellion. In this case, the more conservative side of his Whiggery won out.

Greeley's views were well summarized in a *Tribune* editorial of May 24, 1842. He acknowledged that the Dorr Rebellion "will have done at least one service to the Country in exciting a general inquiry into and discussions of the fundamental principles on which our Political Institutions are based." Greeley believed it called for a reassessment of the Declaration of Independence and the principle that government derived its powers from the consent of the governed. Was this principle subject to limitations? If so, what were the nature and extent of these limitations? Greeley pointed out that restrictions on suffrage already existed. For example, women, minors, and African Americans could not vote. Revealing a less inclusive understanding of democracy than the Dorrites, Greeley asserted that the principles of the Declaration had never been "practically construed to imply that every human being is entitled, from the circumstances that he resides in a certain community and is amenable to its laws, to an equal voice in the making and altering of these laws, nor even to a share in directing the Government."

Throughout the critical months of 1842, Greeley expanded on his views of events in Rhode Island. As he had with the Anti-Rent War, he continued to endorse protest only if it followed constitutional means. Change, he declared, should be effected only "through the action of the State in its organized, recognized capacity—through a Convention regularly called by the Legislature." Greeley opposed the resort to violence and extraconstitutional methods, claiming that Dorr's grievances did not justify a revolution.

He further challenged the Dorrite assumption that "*a major-ity of the People* have an inalienable right to change their form of Government, or establish an entirely new one, at such time and in whatever manner they may choose." A few weeks later, Greeley insisted that the right of the majority to form and alter governments "must have *some* limitations." He explained that the error of Dorr and his followers "lay in confounding the Right of Revolution, which is limited only by the extent of the grievances in which it takes rise, with the right of peacefully changing the Government, which exists only in those whom the existing consti-tution recognises as voters."

Greeley spelled out to his readers what he saw as the insidious implications of the Dorr Rebellion. "Admit it valid," he warned, and "all Courts, all laws, all Constitutions, become the merest frost-work, which the next breath may dissipate, or which a bushel of votes, collected by a peddler on his rounds, may utterly set aside. It cannot be that Free Institutions are so utterly unstable and base-less." Here Greeley seemed to echo his fellow Whig from Illinois, Abraham Lincoln, who had worried in his 1837 Lyceum Address about the mob violence that seemed to be plaguing the country. Greeley suggested that the "fundamental assumption of Dorrism" was also behind the murder of Mormon leader Joseph Smith and the nativist riots in the Southwark area of Philadelphia: "all appear to be based on this very principle."

In 1843, Rhode Island adopted a more liberal constitution. Thomas Dorr returned to the state, was arrested and imprisoned in October for high treason, and was sentenced to life imprison-ment. (Dorr was eventually released by an act of the Democratic legislature in 1845.) Greeley approved of Dorr's sentence, saying, "We must regard the sentence of the Court as a just and righteous one." For Greeley, an important lesson of Whig philosophy had been vindicated as "a conspiracy against the laws of the land, the peace of the nation, the sacredness of individual life and property, that would have been TREASON had it ever risen to the dignity of a temporary success, is for ever laid, and the head and front of this forlorn and desperate enterprise is in the hands of the law of that country he would so foully have outraged. Let his fate be an enduring lesson and a warning to the restless, the dissatisfied and reckless spirit of the times."

V

"Our manifest destiny," announced the *Democratic Review*, "is to overspread the continent allotted by Providence for the free development of our yearly multiplying millions." Editor John L. O'Sullivan's 1845 clarion call for continental expansion resonated throughout the United States in the years thereafter. Americans of the late Jacksonian era focused their outward gaze on Oregon, which had been under joint Anglo-American occupation, and Texas, which had declared its independence from Mexico in 1836. Under the Democratic election slogan of "Fifty-four Forty or Fight," many Americans clamored for a northwest border for Oregon that reached all the way to Alaska.

Like the National Reform movement and the Anti-Rent War, westward expansion highlighted the importance of land for Horace Greeley. Greeley remained unenthused about expansionism in the Pacific Northwest, but acquiesced to the popular demand for Oregon in the North. The politics of expansionism proved far more divisive than the Dorr Rebellion or the New York Anti-Rent War. Because it involved slavery, the combination of Oregon and Texas drove a deep wedge between the North and South. It forced Greeley as a devoted Whig to confront the political implications of the growing Northern distrust of the "slave power."

On a visit to Washington in February 1845, Horace Greeley wrote to his wife that Texas was "the only matter thought of." The annexation of Texas had its roots in John Tyler's accidental presidency. As the vice presidential candidate under the hero of Tippecanoe, Tyler became the nation's leader after William Henry Harrison's untimely death a month after his inauguration. In the early 1830s, Tyler had been a states-rights Democrat from Virginia who became estranged from Andrew Jackson after the nullification controversy. When he became president in 1841, Tyler almost immediately began to alienate his fellow Whigs through a series of vetoes of treasured Whig economic policies. Editor Greeley expressed the Whig disappointment with Tyler, portraying the president as a man who "stood forth an imbittered [sic], implacable enemy of the party which had raised him from obscurity and neglect to the pinnacle of power."

Urged on by Southern supporters like John C. Calhoun, Tyler seized upon the annexation of Texas as a way to unite Democrats and Southern Whigs around a presidential bid in 1844. When Calhoun became secretary of state in 1844, he openly defended not only the annexation of Texas but slavery itself. Southerners supported annexation because it meant the addition of slave territory. Northern Whigs were united against it. For the solid Whig Greeley, annexation also masked a covert Southern attack on the tariff.

The annexation of Texas loomed large as the presidential contest of 1844 approached. The Democrats rejected both Tyler and old party stalwart Martin Van Buren, whom Southerners did not trust. "The question of annexing Texas," Greeley recalled in his autobiography, ". . . had been manipulated as to render many Southern politicians bitterly, actively hostile to Mr. Van Buren, who had taken ground adverse to annexation under the existing conditions." The Democrats instead chose James K. Polk ("Young Hickory") from Tennessee, who ran on a platform of expansionism.

Greeley was in attendance as the Whigs gathered in their national nominating convention in Baltimore on May 1, 1844. His beloved Henry Clay was chosen to bear the standard of the Whig Party. Greeley worked exceptionally hard for Clay that summer, giving speeches on his behalf at political meetings several times a week. Indeed, the thirty-three-year-old editor, according to his friends, worked himself into a state of exhaustion. Greeley complained that his arms had developed painful boils. He and Thomas McElrath published the *Clay Tribune* as a separate sheet, which Greeley considered "one of the most effective daily political journals ever yet issued."

Despite Greeley's efforts, the Whig campaign of 1844 was an uphill struggle. Clay's own vacillations on annexation during the campaign alienated anxious slaveholding Southerners. The vexing issue of slavery posed difficulties for Northern Whigs. The antislavery Liberty

Party nominated James G. Birney as its presidential candidate, and Greeley and other party leaders sought to stop Whig defections to the Liberty Party. Some abolitionists attacked Clay, but Greeley defended him. In an October editorial, "A Word to Antislavery Whigs," Greeley warned that breaking from the Whig Party would lead to "victory for Polk and Texas." In his view, Liberty men were placing "party advantage" ahead of the good of the country.

Still, Greeley was confident that the issues between the parties were clear to the voters and would lead to a Whig victory. Party leaders accordingly attacked Polk as not only an unknown but as a dangerous Locofoco Democrat. They pushed heavily on the tariff during the summer, claiming that the Democrats were not to be trusted. Seeking to expand their electoral base, some Whigs looked toward the nativists. In New York City, an anti-immigrant "Native American" movement was drawing away Whig voters. Yet Greeley resisted these efforts, attacking the religious bigotry of the American Republican Party.

In the fall election, Polk defeated Clay. Birney took enough votes away from Clay in New York to give the Empire State, and hence the election, to the Democrats, who also ran the popular Silas Wright for governor. In the election postmortems, Greeley blamed the Liberty Party for taking votes away from the Whigs. Yet he also attacked the nativists: "The Naturalized Citizens have all been carried for Polk by appeals to their Religious and old-world feelings and prejudices."

VI

After the election of 1844, the Whigs searched for a winning strategy. They stayed united as a party and looked for issues that would distinguish them from the Democrats. By 1846, the Polk administration had given them some ammunition. That summer, congressional Democrats passed the Walker Tariff, which generally lowered tariff duties.

As a Whig editor, Greeley kept up the opposition to the Polk administration, "especially against its dealings with the Tariff question." He hammered hard on the tariff during the summer of 1846, insisting to his protectionist readers that the Democrats were not to be trusted. He argued that Polk's fiscal policy was wrongheaded. Greeley was confident that voters would repudiate the Democrats when their views on the tariff and Texas became more widely known.

In New York, the Whig Party suffered a growing chasm between a progressive, liberal wing led by Thurlow Weed, William H. Seward, and Horace Greeley and a conservative wing represented by James Watson Webb's *Courier & Enquirer*, Greeley's editorial nemesis. The progressives were willing to court black, immigrant, and Liberty Party voters. At the New York constitutional convention of 1846, Greeley supported abolishing the property requirement for black voters: "Let every citizen vote," he wrote. "That is just, equal, liberal, and according to the Declaration of Independence."

The outbreak of the Mexican War in 1846 incited both partisan and sectional conflict. As a Northern Whig, Greeley opposed the war from the beginning. He labeled it "a most unjust and rapacious war, instigated wholly . . . by a determination to uphold and fortify Slavery." Throughout the conflict, the *Tribune* remained stridently antiwar. Greeley worried that the conflict with Mexico would provoke trouble with Great Britain. He also voiced his apprehension of subduing a foreign population in an aggressive war of conquest. The Mexican War might be victorious, Greeley editorialized, and "it may acquire immense accessions of territory; but these victories, these acquisitions, will prove fatal calamities, by sapping the morals of our people, inflating them with pride and corrupting them with the lust of conquest and gold."

The Mexican War, and the accompanying prospect of adding more territory to the United States, helped galvanize a free soil movement in the North aimed at stopping the spread of slavery into the territories. The Liberty Party, led by editors Joshua Leavitt and Gamaliel Bailey, had already laid a foundation. The free soil crusade was strengthened in the mid-1840s by antislavery advocates who had left both major political parties. Democrats were led by the early defection of Representative John P. Hale of New Hampshire, who spoke out publicly against annexation. Hale's supporters organized the Independent Democrats, who, along with antislavery

The *Tribune* editor joins Clay in denouncing the Mexican War. (Courtesy of the Library of Congress)

Whigs, formed the New Hampshire Alliance that sent Hale back to Washington as a U.S. senator. The major impetus to the free soil movement in the North, however, was the "Barnburner" revolt of New York antislavery Democrats led by Van Buren and Silas Wright against the more conservative "Hunker" wing of the state party. Within the Whig Party, Joshua Giddings of Ohio became an early antislavery leader.

The free soil movement crystallized around the Wilmot Proviso of 1846, which called for the prohibition of slavery in any territory acquired in the war with Mexico. Greeley began to agitate for the proviso in the fall of 1846 with editorials like "Freedom Triumphant!" He endorsed it as "a solemn declaration of the United North against the further extension of Slavery under the protection of our Flag."

According to one of Greeley's earliest biographers, the annexation controversy turned the tone of the *Tribune* increasingly against slavery. Articles that depicted the horrors of slavery appeared with more frequency. Some antislavery Northerners had been waiting for the *Tribune* to play a greater role. Charles Sumner, a free-soil

Greeley (last figure on the right) as a Whig opponent of "Mr. Polk's War."
(Courtesy of the Library of Congress)

Whig from Massachusetts, exulted that "the *Tribune* has spoken at last." Yet in late 1847, Greeley retreated a bit from his free soilism to advocate a "No Territory" platform rather than the Wilmot Proviso. Greeley considered the former "the simplest and safest solution to the impending difficulty; if the South will unite on that the whole danger will be averted."

The Free Soil Party was formally established the following summer, when Conscience Whigs, Barnburner Democrats, and Liberty Party men met in Buffalo, New York, in August 1848. Greeley never joined the Free Soil Party, remaining committed to the Whigs. As early as 1842, he had editorialized that Southerners should not believe that "because the Northern Whigs are hostile to Gag-Laws and to Slavery in our own States, that there is any identity of feeling and action between them and the Political Abolitionists." Greeley also insisted that a third party was not the best way to abolish slavery.

As the election of 1848 approached, Greeley remained firmly committed to antislavery. "Human slavery is at deadly feud with the common law, the common sense, and the conscience of mankind," Greeley wrote in January 1848. "Nobody pretends to justify it but those who share in its gains and its guilt." He also maintained that Congress had no right to legalize slavery, as it would not recognize "Polygamy, Dueling, Counterfeiting, Cannibalism or any other iniquity condemned by and gradually receding before the moral and religious sentiment of the civilized and Christian world."

Greeley remained loyal to the party to which he had attached his editorial career, but he saw that the sectional controversy might change the political and electoral landscape. "If Whigs are to be driven to choose between their devotion to the Free Soil principle and their desire of a Whig triumph," Greeley warned, perhaps with his own future in mind, "they will prefer Freedom to Party." During the tumultuous decade of the 1850s, this sentiment would lead many Whigs, including Horace Greeley, into the Republican Party.

Chapter Five

---○---

The Politics
of Antislavery
The 1850s

TWO REVOLUTIONS BRACKETED THE EXPLOSIVE decade of the 1850s. In 1848, liberal and nationalist revolts in France, Germany, and Italy plunged Europe into revolutionary turmoil. In the United States, the end of the Mexican War gave the United States vast new territories that triggered a controversy over slavery in the territories. That year also witnessed less violent but perhaps equally significant political revolutions: antislavery free soilers bolted from both the Whig and Democratic parties, and women's rights advocates met in Seneca Falls, New York, to demand citizen's rights for women. Another revolution brought the 1850s to a close: the election of Republican Abraham Lincoln to the presidency in 1860 set off a wave of secession by seven states of the Lower South.

Horace Greeley played a visible and influential role in American political life between these two watershed years. The *Tribune* was a major conduit through which Americans learned about the European revolutions of 1848. It also became one of the leading voices of the emerging Republican Party during the 1850s. The years between 1848 and 1860, pivotal ones in the political history of the United States, provide perhaps the best opportunity to examine how Greeley's liberalism confronted the problem of slavery.

Once again, Greeley closely reflected the ambivalence so characteristic of antebellum American life. His desire for a new antislavery party was tempered by his devotion to the Whigs. He vigorously fought nativism, yet remained skeptical over the ability of Irish immigrants to assimilate into American society and politics. He supported the rise of the antislavery third party, but urged Illinois Republicans to support Democrat Stephen A. Douglas. As he played a leading role in what he considered the great battle between freedom and slavery, he disavowed, as Lincoln himself did, any intention to interfere with human bondage where it already existed.

I

James Parton called 1848 the "Year of Hope." His optimistic sentiment rested on the outburst of revolutionary ferment in Europe. As it had been in 1789, Paris was once again the epicenter of revolution. On February 24, Parisian crowds forced the abdication of King Louis Philippe and declared France's Second Republic. By June, the revolutionary proletariat in Paris had turned violent, as workers at barricades confronted government forces. In the meantime, the Second Republic pursued radical experiments in republicanism. French republicans created "national workshops" for unemployed workers and abolished slavery in the French West Indies. After the French revolt, Greeley editorialized that the "Emancipation of Europe" had begun.

Inspired by events in France, revolts broke out in Germany and elsewhere. Barricades appeared in the streets of Vienna while the National Assembly meeting in Frankfurt established a liberal constitution for Germany. In April 1849, Louis Kossuth wrote a Hungarian declaration of independence from the Habsburg Empire. Led by Giuseppe Mazzini and Giuseppe Garibaldi, Italians also joined the springtime of hope. Across the channel, a Young Ireland movement led an abortive uprising in 1848, while English authorities turned the other anxious eye to closely watch their own worker Chartists.

American eagerly greeted the revolutions of 1848. A mass meeting in New York in April expressed enthusiasm for the revolutions in Germany, France, and Italy. Many Americans drew comparisons between the various liberal impulses in the Western world. "I find the cause of tyranny and wrong everywhere the same," Margaret Fuller wrote from Rome. "I listen to the same arguments against the emancipation of Italy that are used against the emancipation of our blacks; the same arguments for the spoliation of Poland as for the conquest of Mexico."

Fuller was one of several foreign correspondents who covered the European revolutions for the *Tribune*. Greeley hired European revolutionaries such as Polish republican Adam Gurowski to write for his newspaper. The *Tribune*'s own Charles A. Dana, who had been sent to Europe to cover the uprisings, brought Karl Marx into the orbit of the newspaper's justly famous literary corps. Greeley's most recent biographer justly claims that the *Tribune* became a "significant lens through which Americans saw the radical republicans of Europe." James Parton recalled that Greeley "wrote incessantly on the subject, blending advice with exhortation, jubilation with warning." The *Tribune* editor shared an enthusiasm for the European revolutions with the liberal and progressive wing of the Whig Party.

Of all the European revolutions, Ireland's quest for independence and republican nationhood stirred Greeley's greatest interest. His embrace of Irish nationalism deserves a closer look, for it provides insights into the kinds of political values he brought into the crusade against slavery and his ongoing adjustment to urban, industrial capitalism. Throughout the 1840s and 1850s, Greeley remained interested in and committed to Irish American nationalism.

The Irish American community in New York City had been growing in numbers and strength. As a result of the Great Famine, close to two million Irish men and women left their home country; roughly three out of four headed to the United States. Between 1840 and 1859, the total number of all immigrants coming to America topped four million. Many immigrants of the antebellum era settled in New York, mushrooming the city's population from 313,000 in 1840 to 814,000 in 1860. The notorious Five Points area boasted the city's highest concentration of Irish. There were also many Irish in the Sixth Ward, which Greeley would later represent for a very brief time in the U.S. Congress.

In the early 1840s, the repeal movement was the primary vehicle of Irish nationalism and republicanism in the United States. Repealers sought to nullify the Union of 1801 between Great Britain and Ireland and demanded freedom from English rule and the right of Irish Catholics to sit in Parliament. The movement was led by the Catholic "Emancipator" Daniel O'Connell, who had absorbed the libertarian and egalitarian ideals of the American Revolution. An Irishman writing to the *Tribune* in 1842 described O'Connell as "a man who sacrifices ease and emolument—who has lived only for the redemption, and would readily die, as he has repeatedly proved, for the honor of his and their country." Greeley publicly supported O'Connell and the repeal movement, arguing that the Union was "fraudulent in its inception, carried by intimidation and corruption." Greeley told his readers that England had "by treachery and force obtained the mastery of Ireland." In June 1844, he spoke at a meeting of the Repeal Association in Washington Hall in New York. Later that year, he addressed another gathering of the United Irish Repeal Association in the large saloon at Tammany Hall. Fellow Whig Governor William H. Seward also supported the repeal movement.

The Irish repeal movement brought out a kind of universalism implicit in much of Horace Greeley's political and reform thought. In the Irish quest for independent nationhood, Greeley endorsed what he saw as a universal movement for the Rights of Man. For example, he once referred to the "cause of Ireland and of universal Freedom." Similarly, a Repeal Association in New York resolved that "enjoying the blessings of Free Institutions ourselves, we cannot but sympathize with the oppressed of other lands."

Greeley was also favorably disposed to the constitutional methods of the repealers. O'Connell had spurned the violent tactics of the United Irishmen of the 1790s and in 1846 formally denounced violence as a means of repeal. "Mr. O'Connell," Greeley wrote in praise, "ardently battling for Catholic emancipation, Equal Representation and a Repeal of the Legislative Union, has never dreamed of carrying either of these measures by any other means than through the action of the Imperial Parliament with the assent of the Crown." Greeley emphasized that O'Connell has "earnestly, imploringly striven to curb the fiery temper of his people; to banish every thought of violence and outrage." Greeley drew a stark contrast between O'Connell and the simultaneous occurrence of Dorrite agitation in Rhode Island.

During the revolutionary movements of 1848, a group of young repealers, impatient with O'Connell's limited goals and constitutional methods, broke away and formed a movement called Young Ireland. These Irish radicals rejected constitutional nationalism and returned to the republican goals and violent means of the United Irishmen of the 1790s. Led by Smith O'Brien, Young Ireland attempted an open rebellion in 1848, which was quickly suppressed. Many prominent Young Irelanders escaped to the United States, where they injected Irish republicanism into American cultural politics. An Irish Republican Union meeting in New York called for efforts to "fill Ireland as far as we can, with Military Science and Republican Spirit." Correctly sensing the political capital to be gained, New York Democrats joined Whigs in supporting Irish nationalism. A gathering on the evening of June 5, 1848, at the Tabernacle featured John Van Buren, Theodore Sedgwick, David Dudley Field, and Samuel Tilden.

Greeley continued his advocacy of Irish freedom and nationalism, showing his support of the Irish "Forty-Eighters" in several ways. He had already joined the Irish Relief Committee in 1847. In July 1848, a Provisional Committee of Ireland was organized, with Robert Emmet as president and Greeley as vice president. Opening his columns to the cause of Irish nationalism, Greeley hired the editor of the *Irish World* to write for the *Tribune*. Prominent Irish American William E. Robinson was also on the newspaper's staff. Yet Greeley explained why he refrained from supporting the movement through public speaking: "You see I am a dry speaker, and cannot hope to interest the Irish People, because I can say nothing which they have not heard better said before. What I hope to do is call in some American born, willing to hear, and submit to them a calm, logical statement of some of the grievances of Ireland, in such a way as to induce them to regard her cause more favorably than it has hitherto been regarded by them."

Greeley saw in Young Ireland the same kind of universalism he had supported in the repeal movement. "Without money, munitions, or military leaders," he explained, "they are embarking in a life-and-death struggle with the richest and most powerful aristocracy the world has ever seen. They fight not their own battle only, but that of the poor and down-trodden throughout the civilized world. This entitles them to the warm sympathies and aid of the masses everywhere, and we trust they will not appeal for these in vain." Greeley presented the conflict between England and Ireland in terms of "injustice and oppression on the ruling side" and "degradation and misery on that of the ruled." The Irish peasant was suffering from "centuries of subjugation and wrong which have stamped their impress on his very soul."

In 1848, Greeley also drew attention to the class dimension of Irish nationalism. He affirmed "that the conquest of Ireland by England, with the resulting confiscation of the Irish soil, whereby it is rendered the exclusive property of a few thousands persons . . . is the fundamental cause of Irish destitution and distress." He explained further that Ireland suffers from the inability of the peasants to pay high rents. Yet, once again, Greeley drew away from violent means of protest and expressed a particular fear of class warfare. He warned his readers that "a Social War—a war of class against class—of tenant against landlord, peer against peasant, cot against castle—is the most horrible of all; and even this may be aggravated by the collision of hostile creeds and races." A similar attitude would resurface during the New York draft riots of 1863.

For our purposes, it is significant that Horace Greeley saw Irish American nationalism as part of a larger liberal crusade in the Western world. An announcement for a meeting of Friends of Ireland explained that this meeting is intended to give an impulse to "liberal sentiment respecting Ireland in America and ultimately to liberal action in Great Britain." Similarly, a repeal meeting in 1844 at Washington Hall in New York resolved that "the enlightened spirit of the age is in favor of the extension of liberal principles and the enjoyment of civil and religious freedom." What was encompassed in Greeley's use of the term *liberal* suffused his approach to other pressing issues in mid-nineteenth-century American politics.

In July of the Year of Hope, the first women's rights convention was held in the United States. The Seneca Falls convention culminated almost two decades of feminist agitation grounded in changing gender roles in middle-class society and conflicts over the role of women in the abolitionist movement. Seneca Falls was a rather small and sleepy New York town nestled in a region known for its evangelical fervor. Its reformist atmosphere attracted the abolitionist couple Henry and Elizabeth Cady Stanton, who had moved there in 1848. Earlier, Elizabeth had made a promise to Philadelphia abolitionist Lucretia Mott to form an organization for the rights of women. Under their leadership, the Seneca Falls convention met in the Wesleyan chapel on July 19 and 20, 1848. They were joined by abolitionist Frederick Douglass. The convention passed a Declaration of Sentiments, which included a demand that women be given "the sacred right of elective franchise" as well as a protest against educational and vocational discrimination.

Greeley lent a sympathetic hearing to the movement. The *Tribune* had a history favoring women's rights, and Greeley employed such early feminists as Margaret Fuller and Jane Swisshelm. He personally seemed to value the company of reform-minded women, befriending women like Susan B. Anthony and Antoinette Brown Blackwell. According to one of Greeley's early biographers, Elizabeth Cady Stanton took a matronly interest in the often unkempt Greeley. She would straighten his tie and his pant legs. In a letter to a friend in 1852, though, the temperamentally moderate Greeley confessed he had never been able to attend a "Convention of the advocates of Women's Rights." He stopped short of fully embracing female suffrage. Characteristically, he suggested that economic modernization would be one path to women's rights. The developing of manufacturing would increase the demand for female labor, which would elevate the social position of women.

II

For Greeley, the election of 1848 was perhaps the most important political event of that tumultuous year. Once again, his Whig Party would square off against the Democrats for the presidency. This year, however, was complicated by the increasing sectionalism that had emerged after the Wilmot Proviso. Southern radicals led by John C. Calhoun had become more vocal in their demands to allow slavery and slaveholders in the territories acquired during the Mexican War. Meanwhile, a burgeoning free-soil movement, dedicated to restricting the spread of slavery into the territories, was making strong headway in the North. Indeed, free soil was proving to be a divisive factor within both the Whig and Democratic parties as free soilers struggled with conservatives for party hegemony. Within the New York Democracy, there was a deepening division between free-soil Barnburners led by Martin Van Buren and conservative Hunker Democrats. Within the Whig Party, William Henry Seward and Horace Greeley were among the antislavery leaders.

The free-soil movement spread throughout the North in the late spring of 1848. New York free soilers met in Utica in June 1848. At a meeting of five thousand antislavery Conscience Whigs in Worcester, Massachusetts, Rockwood Hoar—with a good ear for alliterative slogans—suggested that the meeting declare for "free soil, free labor, and free men." This catchphrase would become the rallying cry for antislavery Northerners throughout the 1850s.

The Whigs also had a difficult and divisive route to choosing their presidential candidate for 1848. Early candidates included Mexican War general Winfield Scott; Senator Thomas Corwin of Ohio; Judge John McLean, also from Ohio; and Daniel Webster. But the nomination came down to a contest between perennial candidate Henry Clay and Zachary Taylor, a Louisiana slaveholder and Mexican War hero.

As a New York Whig leader and editor of the influential *New York Tribune*, Greeley played an important role in the politics of nomination. Known mostly for his vocal support of Clay, he was most consistent in his opposition to Taylor. Greeley's partisan activities in 1848 speak not only to his continuing adherence to traditional Whig ideas but also to the growing importance of antislavery free-soil sentiment for Northern Whigs.

Henry Clay had long held ambitions to be president. He had been an unsuccessful National Republican candidate in 1824 and

1832 and the Whig nominee in 1844. During the spring of 1847, Clay considered another run and in July began a tour of the East that mixed politics with a vacation. Clay retained an enormous popularity among Whigs who considered him the embodiment of their principles. Yet many Whigs were reluctant to run him again after so many defeats, most recently in 1844. They also felt that issues like banks, distribution of public lands, and internal improvements no longer had the resonance they once did. After a good deal of private speculation that threatened to hurt the party, his Whig followers urged him to publicly declare his candidacy, which he finally did on April 10, 1848.

The Mexican War had raised the issue of slavery extension, opening the possibility for a Northern Whig candidate. Northern antislavery Whigs, looking for such a man, were urging Clay to come out openly for the Wilmot Proviso. Clay finally addressed the issue of slavery in his Lexington Address of November 13, 1847. In a series of resolutions, Clay offered the Whigs a clear exposition of antiwar principles. After denouncing the calamitous effects of war (Clay would soon lose a son in combat), he attacked President James Polk's administration of the war. In good Whig fashion, Clay maintained that Congress, rather than an imperial president, should decide war aims. He argued additionally that Mexico would be difficult to incorporate into America and that territory should not be acquired just for the sake of slavery. Clay's Lexington Address elicited popular response from Northern Whigs, and its resolutions were adopted at Whig meetings throughout the North.

Throughout 1847 and into 1848, Greeley was a leading figure in the movement among Northern Whigs for a Clay nomination. For example, he arranged for publication of Clay's Lexington Address. The *Tribune* was the major newspaper speaking for Clay in late summer of 1847. One historian considers Greeley "a sort of eastern manager for the Clay candidacy." On November 30, 1847, Greeley wrote Clay about his hope to hold "a great public demonstration" on behalf of the Lexington Address. Greeley was also the leading spirit behind a meeting at Castle Garden in New York that drew about ten thousand Clay supporters in February 1848. New York Whig legislators declared their support in early April 1848, and Greeley assured Clay that they would rally around his name "until the last."

Clay's great rival for the nomination was Zachary Taylor. The Taylor movement was spearheaded by a group of congressional Whigs known as the "Young Indians," mostly Southerners like Alexander Stephens and Robert Toombs of Georgia and William B. Preston and Thomas Flourney of Virginia. First-term congressman Abraham Lincoln also gave his support to the Young Indians. Taylor was appealing as a nonpartisan military hero who could help bury the declining economic issues that were dragging the Whig Party down. Taylor's stock rose rapidly with his victory at Buena Vista in February 1847, a stunning military feat that made him an instant hero. He received support from Clay's enemies in Kentucky, a group that now included John J. Crittenden. New York conservative Whigs, whose editorial spokesman was James Watson Webb at the New York *Courier*, also backed Taylor's nomination.

But by the autumn of 1847, many Northern Whigs had become suspicious of Taylor's nonpartisan candidacy. The general had been proclaiming that he would be a president of the nation rather than a party. Simply put, they wondered how much Taylor was a "real" Whig. In response to these concerns, Taylor issued his "Allison Letter" of April 20, 1848, stating he was a Whig, if not an "ultra" one. This letter first appeared in the New Orleans *Picayune* five days later.

Throughout the battle for the Whig nomination of 1848, Greeley persistently worked to stop a Taylor nomination. He told Clay emphatically that Taylor "cannot be nominated in a Whig National Convention." Capitalizing on the moral outrage of Whigs over the Mexican War, Greeley maintained that it was a mistake to nominate a general "fresh from a war of invasion." In an election, Taylor would alienate Quakers and "peace men." In Greeley's eyes, Taylor was also unreliable on the question of slavery expansion. Taylor took the position—compatible with the views of Southern Whigs—known as "No Territory": the issue of slavery would not arise if the United States did not acquire any new territory. Increasingly attentive to free-soil sentiment, Greeley editorialized that Taylor must come out openly for the Wilmot Proviso to carry New York.

Campaign banner for Whig candidates in 1848. (Courtesy of the Library of Congress)

Greeley also insisted that Taylor was unreliable as a Whig. Many Whigs recalled the mistake of putting John Tyler on the national ticket in 1840. After William Henry Harrison's untimely death, President Tyler vetoed a variety of cherished Whig legislation. Greeley insisted that a Taylor nomination would jettison the support from old Whig counties. In contrast, Winfield Scott, according to the *Tribune* editor, was "not afraid to say he is a Whig and knows what a Tariff is." By insisting on loyalty to traditional Whig principles, Greeley reflected the views of many party leaders that Taylor supporters would abandon party ideals for electoral and patronage success. Greeley wrote that Taylor's friends were the "rotten, run-down, kicked-out and used-up" of both parties. He told Clay that Taylor Whigs "have resolved to throw overboard a good part of our principles so as to make a surer rush for the Spoils." Greeley, for one, did not want "Taylorism" to be "the ruling element in our party."

The Whig national convention convened in Philadelphia on June 7, 1848. Clay believed that Greeley was behind him up to the beginning of the convention. Yet in a letter to Clay on May 29, Greeley shared his fears that the cause had already been lost. Whig leaders in Washington had already decided upon Taylor. Nonetheless, Greeley served as one of Clay's floor managers in Philadelphia along with John Minor Botts of Virginia and James Harlan of Kentucky.

Taylor's forces at the national Whig convention were well organized and energized. On the first ballot, Taylor received 111 votes to Clay's 97, Scott's 43, and Webster's 22. Taylor finally prevailed on the fourth ballot. "We were overborne," Greeley wrote to Clay later that month, "by the immense influence of that central position, and by the combined power of politicians, presses and money."

During the summer of 1848, Greeley remained reluctant to support Taylor: "Thus far, I stand at bay, and have resisted all the clamor of those whose coats turn easy that I ought to raise the Taylor flag. I suppose I shall have to do it in the end, but I am not in any hurry." It was not until September that Greeley openly declared his support for Zachary Taylor. Not coincidentally, this public endorsement occurred after he became a candidate to fill an unexpired term in Congress. Greeley's support for Taylor, how-ever uninspired, was an expression of loyalty to New York Whig leaders.

In explaining his partisan actions during the contest for the Whig nomination in 1848, most historians agree that Greeley saw Clay's candidacy as the "handiest means" to prevent a Taylor nomi-nation. They suggest that Greeley really wanted either of the Ohio candidates, John McLean or Thomas Corwin. John Teesdale, editor of the *Ohio State Journal* and a manager for McLean, wrote that Greeley confessed to Governor William Bebb of Ohio that he sup-ported Clay "in order, if possible to prevent Taylor's nomination."

Supporting this interpretation, historian Michael Holt suggests that Greeley's attempt to make Clay's "Raleigh Letter" a statement of anti-extensionism was not very convincing. Greeley's support for Clay as a means to stop Taylor can be further explained by partisan exigencies in New York. First, Greeley and other New York Whigs, witnessing the divisive split within the New York Democracy be-tween Barnburners and Hunkers over slavery, wanted to avoid a similar schism in their own ranks. Second, Greeley—along with Thurlow Weed and Seward—believed that a Taylor nomination would strengthen Weed's Whig opponents in New York. McLean's friends in New York offered a third explanation: They accused the New York Whig triumvirate of Weed, Seward, and Greeley of shift-ing support away from Taylor in order to put Seward as the vice presidential candidate on a ticket with Clay.

Greeley's opposition to Taylor's nomination reflected a strong belief among many Whigs that the Mexican War hero could not and should not be the standard-bearer of Whig ideals. This is why Greeley stated that the 1848 national Whig convention was "a slaughterhouse of Whig principles." Yet the power of Greeley's free-soil opposition to Taylor the Louisiana slaveholder should not be underestimated. In a letter to a Mr. Wells in May 1848, Greeley provided six reasons why he opposed a Taylor nomination. The first two address slavery. Greeley insisted first that Taylor was a large slaveholder "and has never uttered one word against the infernal system—wherein he differs from Mr. Clay." Second, Greeley re-minded Wells that Taylor was against the Wilmot Proviso.

The importance Greeley was attaching to free-soil sentiment
in 1848 is also evident in a letter to Whig abolitionist congressman
Joshua Giddings of Ohio. "The truth here," Greeley wrote from
New York, "is there is *no* deep devotion to Principle among any
large portion of the American People." Greeley was probably referring to the debate over black suffrage at the 1846 New York Constitutional Convention. The Whigs had been traditional supporters
of civil rights for free blacks, and Greeley noted the "Colorphobia
which prevails so extensively in the ranks of our modern 'Democracy.'" Another reason he was fearful of supporting Taylor was what
it might do to the *Tribune*, testifying to the growing strength of
free-soil sentiment in the North. Nonetheless, at this point in time
Greeley was unwilling to abandon the Whigs for the newly formed
Free Soil Party, though he assured Giddings that he liked its principles. He feared that a third party would help elect the Democratic
candidate, Lewis Cass.

The Free Soil Party was born in Buffalo, New York, in August
1848. Barnburner Democrats who had seceded from the New York
Democracy in June were joined by Conscience Whigs, Liberty
Party men, and black abolitionists such as Henry Highland Garnet,
Charles Remond, and Frederick Douglass. The Buffalo platform
denounced the slave power and called for the federal government "to
relieve itself of all responsibility for the existence and continuance
of slavery." It also called for the abolition of slavery in Washington,
D.C., and its prohibition from the territories. The Free Soil convention nominated Martin Van Buren and Charles Francis Adams,
son of John Quincy Adams. The meeting ended with what would
become a popular slogan for political antislavery: "Free soil, free
speech, free labor, and free men."

The 1848 presidential election thus pitted Whig Zachary
Taylor against free soiler Martin Van Buren and Democrat Lewis
Cass. Greeley supported the principle of the free soilers, but fell
back on the party line to support the Whigs. According to an early
biographer, Greeley "ceased to *oppose* the election of Gen. Taylor,
but would do nothing to promote it." Still maintaining that the
nomination was "unwise and unjust," Greeley nonetheless publicly

endorsed the Taylor ticket at Whig ratification meeting in Vauxhall Gardens in New York on September 27.

Taylor was victorious in the fall election. As a Louisiana slaveholder, he brought back to the Whigs the Southern states of Louisiana and Georgia. The general also won convincing victories in Upper South states—Kentucky, Tennessee, and North Carolina. The Free Soil Party was not so fortunate. In fact, its debut into national politics proved rather discouraging. It won only 10 percent of the national popular vote and just 15 percent in the free states. Van Buren and Adams did not win a single electoral vote.

III

The year 1848 was important to Greeley for another reason, for at the end of the year he was a congressman. In December, he was elected to finish a three-month term for the Sixth Congressional District in New York. The seat in Greeley's district had become vacant when the incumbent congressman was unseated for election fraud. In the nineteenth century, it was not uncommon for newspaper editors to enter electoral politics. James G. Blaine of Maine, for example, a future fellow Republican of Greeley's, began his political career as an editor of the Kennebunk *Journal*.

Greeley joined another freshman Whig congressman who had served in the first session, Abraham Lincoln of Illinois. Greeley wrote daily letters of his activities to the *Tribune*. On December 13, 1848, he introduced a land reform (homestead) bill, a cause dear to his heart. He also backed the building of a railroad across the Isthmus of Panama. Yet his congressional career was controversial and notably undistinguished. Unfortunately, Greeley's fame as a legislator rests upon what James Parton called "the famous Congressional Mileage Expose." Greeley accused members of Congress of charging more for mileage than their trips to and from Washington actually cost. He calculated that this practice had cost the public more than $62,000. Greeley's imputations triggered immediate and fierce responses by his congressional colleagues. One Illinois representative called Greeley's motives "as base, unprincipled and corrupt as ever actuated an individual in wielding his pen for the public press."

Greeley's life away from the *Tribune* and the world of New York politics, whether in the halls of Congress or in his own parlor, was less than satisfying. In 1844, the Greeleys moved from the city to a more rural, secluded home on Turtle Bay on the East River, about two miles from what was then the heart of Manhattan. They later returned to New York City and in 1853 moved to Chappaqua, New York, where he indulged his interests in "agriculture." One observer remarked that the farm had "a fearfully slip shod look."

By many accounts, Greeley's wife Mary continued to be a difficult person. She was seemingly compulsive about cleanliness, perhaps even beyond her own home. She once took the cigar out of the mouth of a passenger on the Staten Island ferry and threw it overboard. One woman reported that she never visited the Greeleys without being insulted by Mary.

Even as Greeley complained about his wife's hypochondria, though, conjugal relations seem to have continued. A son, Arthur Young Greeley, was born in March 1844. Affectionately called "Pickie" by his father, young Arthur was befriended by the childless Margaret Fuller, who was often a visitor at the Greeley household. Greeley spoiled Pickie, who seemed to provide one source of intimacy for the father. "He and I," Greeley once wrote, "are very needful to each other." Tragically, Pickie died from cholera in July 1849. A grieving Greeley confided to a friend that "few parents have lost children [who] were more calculated to fix all hearts than our boy."

Another Greeley son, Raphael, died in 1857. Sadly, childhood death plagued the Greeleys, as it did many families in antebellum America. Out of nine children conceived in that period, only two survived. Horace sought other friendships, particularly with Fuller, and undoubtedly found solace by pouring himself into his work. After 1848, keeping the Whig Party alive was a major challenge.

IV

The demise of the Whig Party between 1848 and 1855 occupies a central place in the complex and turbulent political history of the 1850s. The intensifying controversy over slavery played the most direct role in the fall of the Whigs. Southern and Northern Whigs had lost their vital sectional center. In addition, intraparty conflicts within states and between sections, personal rivalries, and a diminution of visible differences with the Democrats contributed to the dissolution of the party. As the editor of an important Whig newspaper and a close political associate of William H. Seward and Thurlow Weed, Greeley's fortunes were closely tied to the Whig Party. He would become one of many Whigs whose antislavery convictions brought them into the new Republican Party.

Zachary Taylor, upon assuming the presidency in 1849, wanted to broaden the Whigs into a more inclusive and nationalist party. He nevertheless faced a very divided party as intraparty conflicts persisted after the elections. In New York, Whigs were torn between an antislavery wing—the Conscience Whigs, led by Seward, Weed, and Greeley—and the more conservative Cotton Whigs, who gathered behind Vice President Millard Fillmore. Seward was in the ascendancy in the Taylor administration—an important fact, since patronage was a key issue in these intraparty squabbles. Greeley was critical of Taylor, once claiming that the president did not "know himself from a side of sole-leather in the way of statesmanship." Like other Whigs, Greeley was angry at what he saw was a virtual abandonment of traditional Whig programs.

President Taylor wanted to admit California directly as a state, due to the explosion of population triggered by the Gold Rush of 1849. Viewing the sectional controversy over slavery with growing alarm, he began to take steps that led to the Compromise of 1850. Taylor believed that skipping California's territorial stage would avoid confronting the troublesome question of slavery in the territories and therefore preserve Whig harmony.

Sectional tensions peaked in 1850. Young Southern followers of John C. Calhoun and radical free soilers in the North were the extremists. Southern radicals met in convention in Nashville in June to insist on the right of slaveholding Southerners to take their property into the territories. In this volatile political environment, Northern Whigs had to not only appease their Southern colleagues but also watch the growing strength of free-soil movements in their own states. A divided and hence weakened party would be less able to compete successfully with the Democrats on both national and local levels.

Seward's allies wanted some version of the Wilmot Proviso to be put into any compromise plan. A compromise package engineered by Greeley's idol Henry Clay was proposed in January 1850. California would be admitted as a free state, while the rest of the Mexican cession would be organized as a territory (New Mexico and Utah) with no mention of slavery. The United States would assume the Texas debt, while New Mexico would receive the disputed land on its border with Texas. To appease Northerners, Clay proposed that the slave *trade*—but not slavery itself—be abolished in Washington, D.C. To appease Southerners, a new, more stringent fugitive slave law was included.

"This Congress must not adjourn without organizing New Mexico and shutting out Texas somehow," Greeley wrote Seward, "and I shall go hard for Clay's log-roll if something better is not put ahead of it." Clay's compromise package was opposed by President Taylor, who had his own plan. Yet Taylor died in July, removing one of the obstacles to compromise. When Clay left Washington in failing health that summer, the compromise forces fell to Stephen A. Douglas, Democratic senator from Illinois. With skillful political maneuvering, Douglas was able to get a final package approved by Congress.

Characteristic of his temperamental moderation and prefiguring his response to the secession crisis of 1860–1861, Greeley vacillated on the compromise. He denounced it early in the year, calling it "gross incompetency" and "flagrant treachery." He was also critical of Daniel Webster's March 7 speech urging sectional conciliation. Yet Greeley tempered his opposition when Fillmore became president. In late July, Greeley called the proposal a "fair and equal compromise on the questions on which the North and the South are at issue."

The debate over the Compromise of 1850 only deepened the division among New York Whigs. Fillmore and his conservative followers sought to curb Seward's influence in the Taylor administration. In addition, the compromise had created a new Union Safety Committee, made up largely of conservative New York merchants, that threatened to draw conservatives away from the Whigs.

Intraparty conflicts came to a head at the New York State Whig convention in September 1850. To help secure Seward's leadership role, Greeley turned against the compromise and Fillmore. The conservatives bolted at this convention. Following the lead of Francis Granger, who had a mane of silver hair, they became known as the "Silver Gray Whigs." Greeley's experience at the 1850 Whig state convention turned him more against slavery. He disliked the state party platform that called for acquiescence to the 1850 compromise, an attitude that incurred the wrath of New York's conservative Whigs.

As the Whigs approached the 1852 election, three viable candidates—Millard Fillmore, Daniel Webster, and Mexican War hero Winfield Scott—sought the party's nomination for president. Determined to achieve the highest political prize, which had always eluded him, Webster would brook no opposition to the compromise or to the South. Many believed that Webster promoted the Union Safety Committee for his own personal advantage even if it hurt the party.

Scott was the choice of Weed and Seward, though Greeley did not hold Scott in high estimation and distrusted his nativism. Yet by February 1851, Greeley knew that Scott would be the inevitable Whig choice. Like Zachary Taylor in 1848, Scott was a popular military figure. Moreover, he had no record on the Compromise of 1850, which made him an attractive candidate.

Even as the New York Whigs were rent by division, Greeley remained loyal to his party and to Seward and refused to join the Free Soil Party. Yet the Whigs faced an uphill battle in 1852. "Our

State is certain," Greeley warned, "unless our Silver Grays behave worse than Judas Iscariot and Benedict Arnold ever knew how to." Economic issues seemed less salient after the return to economic prosperity in the early 1850s. Moreover, prohibition had emerged as a potent political issue that could also split the party. In their national party platform in 1852, the Whigs accepted the finality of the compromise. But Greeley was unmoved. On this position, Greeley proclaimed, "We defy it, execrate it, spit upon it." Comments like these, coming from such a prominent Whig editor, embarrassed the Silver Gray Whigs in upstate New York.

With such internecine divisions, the Whigs went down to a huge defeat in the fall elections. Democrat Franklin Pierce defeated Scott by 254 to 42 electoral votes, rendering that presidential election the worst defeat in the party's history. New York Whigs won only eleven of thirty-three congressional seats.

The Whig Party was clearly in a downward spiral. In the early 1850s, new issues arose with the potential to draw clear distinctions between Whigs and Democrats. The Whigs, however, did not benefit from this opportunity. Rather, a number of small parties devoted to prohibition, nativism, and anti-partyism rose to challenge the Democrats. From Greeley's perspective at the time, there was less and less reason for him to cling to the Whigs. First, they remained uncommitted to stopping the spread of slavery and resisting the demands of slaveholders. Second, Greeley faced increasing competition from other Whig editors in New York City such as James Watson Webb and Henry J. Raymond.

Greeley remained disillusioned with the Whig Party throughout 1853, even changing the name of the *Whig Almanac* to the *Tribune Almanac*. "Our faith in the wisdom of the habitual leaders of the Whig party is weak," Greeley acknowledged in 1854, "but our confidence in the intelligence and uprightness of the Whig masses is unbounded." That year, another sectional issue would explode on the political landscape. While it would ultimately drive more nails into the Whig coffin, it offered Greeley, other antislavery Whigs, and free-soil Democrats a new and ultimately successful party option.

V

The Republican Party was initially formed in the aftermath of the Kansas-Nebraska Act of 1854 from a coalition of several antislavery constituencies: Free Soil Party men, Conscience Whigs, free soil Democrats, and Liberty Party abolitionists. It was later joined by Know-Nothings, prohibitionists, and German immigrants. Six years later, in 1860, the Republican candidate Abraham Lincoln would win the presidency. Lincoln's election, of course, then touched off a successful secessionist effort in the Deep South that led quickly and precipitously toward civil war. Horace Greeley played an influential role in the rapid rise of the Republican Party in the mid-1850s. As a political leader, he helped transition former Whigs into Republicans.

Roots of the new third party can be found in the Northern responses to the Fugitive Slave Law of 1850, which had been a crucial component of the compromise for Southerners. Designed to appease the demands of slaveholders, the Fugitive Slave Law was a harsh measure for its victims. To encourage the rendition of escaped slaves from the South, the law denied its victims trial by jury. The accused captured fugitive would be presented to a federal commissioner rather than a judge. This commissioner would receive $10 if he ordered the return of the captive to slavery and $5 if he ordered his or her release—an incentive weighing heavily against the accused. The Fugitive Slave Law infuriated Northerners, rapidly increasing antislavery and anti-Southern sentiment. Ralph Waldo Emerson labeled it a "filthy law." Greeley called it a "gross and unpardonable exercise of tyrannical power, a criminal outrage upon the inalienable rights of man." The *Tribune* editor thought it both unconstitutional and immoral. Speaking for many Northerners, Greeley explained that "we cannot and will not do aught tending to reenslave a human being who has escaped from his alleged owner or owners."

For Greeley, the Fugitive Slave Law was objectionable because it made the North complicit in slaveholding: "Every instance of Slavery Extension under our National flag, or of slave-catching in

Free States, argues that our disclaimers are false, and that we are really accomplices and bailiffs of the slaveholder for a paltry share of his unjust gains." This kind of thinking reflected a growing belief that slavery, if unchecked, would become a national institution. "Against all requirements of complicity on our part in the sin and shame of chattelizing Man," Greeley explained, "the conscience of the North instinctively revolts, and the desire of her people to maintain an unsullied reputation continually protests."

Throughout the North, the revulsion against the Fugitive Slave Law led to acts of open resistance to federal authorities. In Boston in 1851, slave catchers arrested a fugitive slave named Shadrach. Before his hearing, a group of African American men broke into the courtroom, overpowered the authorities, and stole him away to freedom. Several Northern states passed personal liberty laws, which made enforcement of the Fugitive Slave Law especially difficult. As might be expected, however, Greeley shied away from these kinds of (often violent) opposition to constituted authority. In June 1854, he could go only so far as to urge that fugitive slave cases be tried by juries as an improvement.

The Kansas-Nebraska Act sparked the formation of the Republican Party. In January 1854, Senator Stephen A. Douglas introduced a bill for the organization of the territories of Kansas and Nebraska. On the controversial issue of slavery, Douglas claimed that the citizens of the territory would decide on slavery before statehood. This principle was often called "squatter sovereignty" or "popular sovereignty," a term invented by Democratic senator Lewis Cass of Michigan in the election of 1848. This doctrine implicitly, and later explicitly, overturned the Missouri Compromise by allowing slavery to spread north of the 36-degree 30-minute parallel. Douglas's Nebraska bill raised a storm of protest, as Northerners saw it as a repudiation of a sacred agreement between the North and South. Greeley regarded "this Nebraska movement of Douglas and his backers as one of measureless treachery and infamy." He protested it as "an act of deliberate bad faith, impelled by the most sordid motives and threatening the most calamitous results." With the backing of Southerners and the Democratic Pierce administration, the Kansas-Nebraska Act became law in May.

Greeley assailed the act in a *Tribune* editorial of June 1, 1854: "One million miles of Territory, heretofore shielded FOREVER from Slavery by a bargain, forced by the South upon a reluctant and struggling North . . . has been opened to slaveholding immigration and settlement, and so exposed to be brought into the Union as Slave States." He joined other antislavery Northerners in seeing the measure as "a desperate struggle of Freedom against Slavery." He excoriated Douglas, calling him a "lying little villain" and a "miserable creature with his impudent, brazen sophistry." Once again, Greeley saw an aggressive and predatory slave power seeking to nationalize slavery. He detected in Douglas's bill a plan for "Nebraska conspirators to carry out their schemes and reduce the North to submission to slave-drivers."

For the next few years, Kansas would become a genuine battleground between slavery and freedom. Speaking before the Senate, Seward promised that "we will engage in competition for the virgin soil of Kansas, and God give the victory to the side that is stronger in numbers as it is right." Proslavery settlers from Missouri crossed the border into Kansas, while free-state emigrants arrived from New England and the Old Northwest.

Greeley joined Eli Thayer and his New England Emigrant Aid Company to financially assist antislavery settlers in moving to the territory. Along with a young Frederick Law Olmsted, Greeley helped purchase a howitzer to be sent to Kansas. The *Tribune* became a leading antislavery voice in the struggle over Kansas. It serialized an antislavery novel, *The Kansas Emigrants*, written by Boston abolitionist Lydia Maria Child, and the newspaper's office openly collected money for the cause. "Bleeding Kansas" became a rallying cry for the new Republican Party. In May 1856, Greeley claimed that "the one question on which all earnest opponents of the Slave Power are united and determined is the Kansas Question." To subjugate the territory to slavery, in his opinion, "would expose the American Union to the execrations of the liberal, just and humane throughout the world."

During the spring and summer of 1854, the Kansas-Nebraska Act unleashed a flurry of anti-extensionist sentiment in the North. Anti-Nebraska meetings drew free soil Whigs, Democrats, and

others into fusion efforts—cooperative endeavors to elect free soil
candidates regardless of party. Greeley supported these early efforts
at fusion. "Anti-Nebraska and anti-rum," he wrote Indiana Whig
Schuyler Colfax, "ought to unite Whigs and Free soilers and carry
your state this fall. Try to bring it about." In the *Tribune* as well,
Greeley proclaimed, "We advocate co-operation and fusion. We
maintain that the only policy of the sincere friends of freedom, and
of those who are determined to resist the aggressions of Slavery, is
to unite in solid phalanx and so make their efforts tell."

Greeley played a visible role as the Republican Party established its national foundations. One of his friends from the land
reform movement, Alvan Bovary, took the lead in one of the first
Republican organizations in Ripon, Wisconsin. In May 1854, a few
New Yorkers led by editor A. N. Cole formed a new political party,
and Greeley suggested the name "Republican," as "it will sound
both Jeffersonian and Madisonian, and for that reason will take
well." He explained further that "some simple name like *Republican* would more fitly designate those who had united to restore our
Union to its true mission of champion and promulgator of Liberty
rather than propagandist of Slavery."

Greeley also supported political fusion under the Republican
banner in New York. State Republican leaders called for a meeting
at Saratoga Springs on August 16, 1854. Greeley called it "one of
the most important political assemblages New-York has ever seen."
He pushed hard for a prohibition plank for the new party's platform.
Greeley had hoped to be put on an electoral ticket as candidate for
governor or lieutenant governor, but was spurned by Weed, who
confessed to never having understood some of Greeley's political
moves. "With all his ability," New York Republican and future secretary of state Hamilton Fish said more negatively, "he has a crack
across his brain that amounts to little short of derangement and will
destroy anything which he may be allowed to lead." Despite this
personal setback, Greeley contributed to a Republican mass meeting in the Tabernacle in New York City in September 1855 to elect
local delegates to the Syracuse meeting. Some of the older Whigs
were suspicious of Greeley's new political venture.

Greeley traveled to Washington in the winter of 1855–1856 to
help elect Republican Nathaniel Banks as Speaker of the House,

constantly writing letters back to the *Tribune*. During this stay in Washington, Representative Albert Rust, a Democrat of Arkansas, who was angered by one of Greeley's editorials, physically assaulted Greeley. Like Senator Charles Sumner in May 1856, Greeley was attacked with a heavy cane. Fortunately, Greeley was not hurt, as bystanders on the street intervened.

In February 1856, Greeley attended the national meeting of Republicans in Pittsburgh, which aimed to organize "a National party, based upon the principle of Freedom." Greeley delivered a speech at this convention inviting others to unite against the spread of slavery.

The transition from Whiggery to Republicanism was not the only political change Greeley made during the 1850s. He also broke off his association with Seward and Weed. During the Compromise of 1850, Greeley had grown increasingly hostile to the Taylor administration and berated Seward for his close connection to the president. He was angry that Weed and Seward were courting Henry J. Raymond and the *New York Times* for their patronage. By 1853, he was complaining that Seward was giving his speeches to the *Times* rather than the *Tribune*. On November 11, 1854, Greeley wrote a private letter to Seward dissolving the partnership "of the political firm of Seward, Weed, & Greeley by the withdrawal of the junior partner." He claimed that he was formally read out of the Whig Party by an editorial in Weed's Albany *Evening Journal* and offered several instances where he felt cheated or unrewarded financially. Greeley was humiliated that Weed had refused to support him for governor and had instead put Raymond on the ticket as lieutenant governor. Yet the three men worked together in the New York Republican Party. In 1858, Greeley confessed to Schuyler Colfax that, although he liked Weed "very much as a man," he had "ceased to follow his lead as a politician."

VI

Attempting to explain the success of the Republican Party, historian Eric Foner has argued that its ideology of free soil, free labor, and free men reflected the deepest hopes and fears of Northern middle-class society in the 1850s. As a newspaper editor, Horace

Greeley made the *Tribune* one of the most influential voices of the Republican ideology. Among its most faithful adherents, Greeley also reveals the ambivalences and ambiguity that would plague Northern Republicanism throughout the Civil War era.

The Republican Party of the 1850s was *antislavery* rather than *abolitionist*. Until the Civil War, the central goal of the party was to stop the spread of slavery into the new territories. "The Republican movement is defensive, not aggressive," Greeley stated in 1856; "conservative of Freedom, rather than destructive of Slavery." As he explained further in 1858, Republicans "believe that Slavery should be restricted to the States now upholding it, and that all the remaining Territories of the Union should be consecrated to Free Labor and Free Men." Greeley joined other Republicans in insisting that Congress had no power to interfere with slavery where it already existed. "It has *power* over the question of planting Slavery in Kansas," he editorialized; "it has no power over, consequently no responsibility for, its perpetuation in Carolina."

Nonetheless, Republicans like Greeley were vehement in their denunciations of slavery. The standard for judging the South's "peculiar institution" was the Republicans' core belief in "free labor," a system in which one was free to sell one's own labor as a commodity in a market economy. Eric Foner argues that the glorification of free labor was "an affirmation of the superiority of the social system of the North—a dynamic, expanding capitalist society, whose achievements and destiny were almost wholly the result of the dignity and opportunities which it offered the average laboring man." After decades of trumpeting Whig notions of improvement, Greeley fully embraced the Republican ideology of free labor. "Enslave a man," he argued, "and you destroy his ambition, his enterprise, his capacity." Greeley insisted that permanent and progressive prosperity could only rest on the basis of free labor. Freedom in Kansas would therefore be dangerous to slavery in Missouri "by showing the superior thrift, energy, comfort, and progress of free over Slave Labor."

Using free labor to gauge the status and progress of society, Republicans engaged in a relentless attack on the slaveholding South. They portrayed the Southern states in stark contrast to the North and as antithetical to the values of free labor. In an editorial on the struggle over Kansas, Greeley captured this Republican critique of the South: "Crowded cities, populous villages, smiling farms, churches, school-houses, growing prosperity, universal education, continual advancement in wealth, intelligence, virtue and happiness, on the one hand, and decay, dilapidation, sterility, ignorance, brutality, pauperism, vice, wretchedness, and the tendency forever toward the worse, on the other." Republicans also depicted the South as an aristocratic social order dominated by planters. "In every Southern State," Greeley explained in 1857, "the planters have been everything, and the laboring men, merchants, mechanics, professional men, nothing." As a consequence of the domination of plantations, the South lacked towns "in which the advocacy of free labor could organize itself." During the 1850s, Greeley attacked the South in other ways as well. He claimed that slave communities were more prone to lynch law. Even the press of the South was "without enterprise, without the news, without original matter, and with nothing in it more interesting than the advertisements of fugacious negroes."

Republican leaders like Greeley focused in particular on the damage slavery inflicted on nonslaveholding whites who were "born and bred under the debilitating atmosphere of Slavery." Greeley explained that the South's peculiar institution "has eaten out their life's life, put its brand upon their foreheads, clothed them in rags, sent them away empty, blighted their minds, quenched their hopes and made them the contempt and derision of the very slaves themselves." Republicans often warned that a class war would engulf the South. In a *Tribune* editorial of November 10, 1858, Greeley insisted that the real struggle in the South would be "not so much between the whites and the blacks as between the great mass of poor whites, whose only means of rising in the world, their labor, is made disgraceful by the existence of Slavery, and the few rich slaveholders enabled to live in idleness and luxury by means of that institution."

The "irrepressible conflict" about which Seward and other Republicans spoke was cast as a contest between two distinctive and contrasting civilizations. What made the territorial question so explosive was that it was the current battleground between freedom and slavery. Since Republicans believed that this battle could determine the future of the United States, they spoke openly of their fear that slavery could spread to the North as well.

They assumed that slavery was, as Greeley stated it, "essentially, necessarily aggressive." As such, geographical expansion was necessary for slavery to survive. "Slavery in the old States," Greeley explained, "has in a generation been kept vital and aggressive by means of successive additions of territory, whereby slaves were rendered valuable and slave-breeding profitable; and that Slavery would have died out ere this, after becoming an intolerable burden to the masters." These expansionist dynamics, Republicans believed, were behind Southern filibustering efforts in the Caribbean and Central America during the 1850s. "The South desires now to purchase Cuba," Greeley warned, "to obtain possession of Hayti [sic], to conquer Mexico, to add the British and French West Indies to the new Slave Republic." An aggressive proslavery faction eagerly advocated the reopening of the African slave trade. The end result, Republicans repeatedly warned, would be the nationalization of slavery. "If we will have a slaveholding ascendancy," Greeley maintained, "if we will extend Slavery into new territories, if, divesting it of its purely local character, we will elevate it to the dignity of national law . . . that is what the slaveholders are aiming at and demanding."

Greeley connected an attack on Northern Democrats to his support of Republicanism, accusing them of being spineless sycophants of the Southern slaveholders. The slave power, he explained, was "backed by northern traitors and doughfaces who dare to perpetuate the extremist crimes against liberty in the name of Democracy." He believed that the slaveholders were secure "in the belief that the masses of the Democratic party can be brought by doughface leaders to aid in the extension of Slavery." In 1856, he concluded that the Democrats therefore "cannot be made anything else than a party for the extension of Slavery and the subjugation of Freedom."

The Republican Party of the 1850s contained a spectrum of racial views, from radical visions of freedom and civil equality to a conservative support for colonization. In some ways, the Republicans did challenge the pervasive racism of the mid-nineteenth century. Yet they trod the racial ground carefully because they were most eager to put together a winning political coalition.

Strategically, Republicans often focused on the dangers slavery posed to white men. Greeley himself recognized that "there are some among us who do not view the matter as altogether a negro question, but believe that Slavery is a far more fatal and consuming curse to the white than it ever could be to the black, and if for that reason alone, would fain see it swept out of existence." Greeley tended to look at race from the Whiggish perspective of "improvement." In 1855, he wrote in the *Tribune* that, as a class, African Americans were "indolent, improvident, servile, and licentious." Yet two years later he editorialized that "there is no reason to believe that, if afforded fair play, the protection of the laws, and opportunities for industry and education, free Negroes might not make useful citizens." Greeley's own ambivalence on the race question reflected the larger ambiguity within the Republican Party that would haunt them during the Civil War and Reconstruction.

The larger worldview of Republicans in the 1850s did extend beyond slavery. As exponents of a free labor ideology, Republicans incorporated notions of economic improvement that had lain at the heart of Whiggery. The Republican platforms of 1856 and 1860 included planks on a Pacific railroad, homesteads, tariffs, and harbor and river improvements. With a vision of the West with available public lands, diversified economic development, and a transcontinental railroad, Greeley became even more of an enthusiastic Republican. Considering the long-standing importance he placed on land, Greeley saw a homestead law "as the great legislative antidote to the fearful tendency of our time to a deluge of Pauperism." He reiterated that it would diminish poverty "by drawing off to the new lands the more active, energetic, hopeful class who now stand between these and employment."

VII

The Republican Party to which Greeley attached himself faced a number of challenges. First and foremost was Democratic dominance. From 1853 to 1861, Democrats occupied the White House and controlled the Supreme Court. Within the party, Southern slaveholders exercised a power disproportionate to their numbers.

Furthermore, Republicans had to build the institutional framework of a political party out of a heterogeneous coalition. And from 1854 to 1856, they had to contend with the rise of the Know-Nothings.

Nativism—a general hostility to foreigners and a particular dislike of Irish Catholics—had firm roots in the antebellum period. In July 1854, the American Party was founded as a political vehicle for nativism. Intended to be a secret society, the party's members were to claim, if asked about the party, that they "knew nothing." The American Party sought to curb the influence of immigrants, particularly Irish Catholics, on U.S. government. The Know-Nothings, as they came to be called, rose quickly in 1854 and 1855, capturing large majorities in such states as Massachusetts and Pennsylvania. In the political chaos of the mid-1850s, they provided a way station for conservative Whigs and anti-Nebraska men.

In New York, for example, conservative Hunker Democrats and the Silver Gray Whigs led the Know-Nothings. Nativism posed a peculiar dilemma for Republicans. On the one hand, fusion with the Know-Nothings was attractive, for they offered a potentially large number of voters. On the other hand, nativism offended the liberal sensibilities of reformers like Horace Greeley.

Greeley opposed the Know-Nothings. "To Native Americanism in every form," he contended, "we are constitutionally averse, declaring it at war with the fundamental principles of our National existence. We recognize the man who lives besides us, pays taxes, and is willing to help defend the country if assailed, as our equal before the law, and fairly entitled to all the franchises and immunities of citizenship, no matter where he was born nor what may be the color of his skin." In 1854, he wrote Schuyler Colfax denouncing nativism as "our traditional, implacable enemy." Anti-Catholic and anti-immigrant prejudice violated Greeley's sense of political equality. He pointed out the "incompatibility of such systematic proscription with the genius of republican institutions, which demands equal opportunities and privileges for all." Anticipating the findings of modern historians, Greeley also recognized that the Know-Nothings were capitalizing on the partisan decay and chaos of the mid-1850s: "It is but one of the many forms of protest against the corruption of party politics, and especially against the deep treachery of the leaders of the Nebraska party to the vital principles of Democracy."

Despite his hostility to the Know-Nothings, however, Greeley expressed a good deal of apprehension over Irish Catholic newcomers. "Our immigrant population is deplorably clannish, misguided, and prone to violence," he once complained. Like many New York Republicans, Greeley disproved of the Irish affinity toward the Democratic Party. He claimed that "Irish associations to influence elections, Irish clanship, Irish claims to office, are all wrong, and Irish browbeating and club-handing at the polls are atrocious." Greeley's vision was more assimilationist, getting Irish immigrants out of taverns and into public schools where they could be properly indoctrinated with "American" Protestant, middle-class values. In this way, his ambiguous views on ethnicity were not dissimilar to those on race.

VIII

Prone to hyperbole, Horace Greeley called the presidential election of 1856 "a canvass destined to form a memorable epoch in our Nation's history." The Whigs, no longer a real force in national politics, nonetheless held their last convention and nominated Millard Fillmore. The Democrats put forth James Buchanan, an older Jacksonian politico from Pennsylvania. William H. Seward emerged as the leading Republican candidate, though he was an anathema to the Know-Nothings due to his previous support of New York Catholics. Greeley was leaning toward John McLean of Ohio and Speaker of the House Nathaniel Banks of Massachusetts. Another name often mentioned was the explorer and California veteran John C. Fremont, the son-in-law of Democratic senator Thomas Hart Benton.

On June 6, 1856, Greeley threw his support behind Fremont in a *Tribune* editorial. Admitting that Fremont was young, Greeley maintained that he "has done more service, braved more peril, and achieved more reputation, than any man of his years now living." Importantly, Fremont had also helped make California a free state and had not alienated anyone in the nativist controversy. Greeley

Greeley supports John C. Fremont for the first Republican presidential
nomination in 1856. (Courtesy of the Library of Congress)

worked at the national Republican convention that year in Philadelphia to line up support for "the Pathfinder," who did get the
nomination. He campaigned furiously through editing, speaking,
and publishing a short biography of Fremont.

In the election, Buchanan beat Fremont with 45.3 percent of
the popular vote. Nevertheless, Greeley remained optimistic. The
Republicans carried eleven of the sixteen free states. "I think we
have no reason to be discouraged," he wrote to Schuyler Colfax,
"we have made a great beginning." Events during the next four years
would help fulfill Greeley's hopes, even as they plunged the nation
toward secession and war.

In March 1857, the Supreme Court handed down its fateful
Dred Scott decision. Dred Scott was a slave who sued for freedom
on the grounds that his residence in both a free state (Illinois) and
a free territory (Minnesota) had made him a free man. Also at issue
in his case was the power of Congress to outlaw slavery in the territories. The Court, led by Chief Justice Roger B. Taney, dismissed
Scott's case on the grounds that, as a slave and a black man, he
was not a citizen and therefore could not sue in federal court. Even
more devastating to Republicans, Taney declared the Missouri
Compromise unconstitutional and insisted that neither Congress
nor a territorial legislature could prohibit slaveholders from entering
with their peculiar property.

Republicans across the North were outraged and not only because the Supreme Court had essentially declared their nonexten-

sion platform unconstitutional. "This decision, we need hardly say," Greeley editorialized, "is entitled to just so much moral weight as would be the judgment of a majority of those congregated in any Washington barroom." The *Tribune* editor attacked *Dred Scott* from the moment it appeared as "a violent and ferocious attack on the rights of human nature." For months, his newspaper carried editorials railing against the decision. In one, Greeley insisted that Chief Justice Taney "seems to have totally forgotten the functions of a Judge, and to have relapsed into the character of an eager, artful, sophistical, Jesuitical, lying advocate—for the suppression of the truth is lying, to all intents and purposes."

If neither Congress nor a territorial legislature could prohibit slavery, was popular sovereignty still a viable option? This was one of the problems emanating from the *Scott* decision that faced Democratic senator Stephen A. Douglas as he went up for reelection in 1858. "The political excitement in this State is tremendous," wrote a *Tribune* correspondent from Illinois in October 1858. Douglas had endeared himself to free soilers in the North by breaking from the Buchanan administration over the Lecompton Controversy. In 1857, proslavery settlers in Kansas had convened a constitutional convention, which was boycotted by antislavery free-staters. This convention proceeded to draft a proslavery constitution that was essentially foisted on Kansans without a fair vote. The Democratic president seized upon the Lecompton Constitution as the basis for calling for Kansas's admission into the Union and made it a test of Democratic Party orthodoxy. Caught between his partisan loyalties and the wishes of his home state of Illinois, Douglas had rebuked the Lecompton Constitution and broke from Buchanan.

A number of eastern Republicans, including Greeley, Henry Wilson of Massachusetts, and Samuel Bowles, editor of the Springfield (Massachusetts) *Republican*, thought that Republicans in Illinois should support Douglas. Yet their efforts during February and March were rebuffed by Republican leaders in Illinois who did not trust Douglas and further argued that they could elect a Republican since the Democrats had been divided by the Lecompton Controversy. Instead, they nominated Abraham Lincoln.

Greeley in particular came under attack by Illinois Republicans over this affair. "I like Greeley," remarked Lincoln, but added that he "thinks he intends right, but I think he errs in this hoisting up of Douglas, while he gives me a downward shove." Lincoln's law partner and political supporter William Herndon considered Greeley "not fit for a leader. He is capricious, crotchety, full of whims, and as wrong-headed as a pig." Greeley gradually backed off from his support of Douglas, though he was miffed by the rejection of his advice. The experience left a bitter taste in the mouths of Illinois Republicans too, which would resurface at the national convention two years later.

After Douglas defeated Lincoln in the Illinois senatorial election of 1858, Greeley attempted to explain his actions in a *Tribune* editorial. Eastern Republicans thought it was best to support those Democrats "who, defying the seductions of Patronage and the frowns of Power, had resisted from first to last the passage of the Lecompton and English bills." This strategy, he explained, had led them to support Douglas's effort to return to the Senate. "In all this," Greeley admitted, "we may have been wholly wrong, and our Illinois friends entirely right." Greeley alluded to threats that Republicans in the Northwest might boycott the *Tribune* that he found regrettable.

IX

The demands of partisan politics and newspaper editing, along with the impending crisis over slavery, tired Greeley. For a respite, he decided he would take a trip to see California. On May 9, 1859, he left New York on a transcontinental trek. The narrative of this trip was published as *An Overland Journey* in 1860. One of Greeley's major goals was to scout out a route for a transcontinental railroad, a project he considered "the grandest enterprise of the age." Greeley traveled with two other journalists, Albert D. Richardson of the Boston *Journal* and Henry Villard of the Cincinnati *Commercial*.

On June 6, Greeley arrived in the recently founded city of Denver, where he stayed at the Denver House Hotel. True to the image of the frontier, the hotel lacked mattresses and pillows. Greeley's letters narrated the familiar dangers of travel, including lost luggage and uncomfortable and unsanitary accommodations on his sleeping berth. In Utah, Greeley stopped to interview Mormon leader Brigham Young. Entering California, he hired a carriage driver, perhaps not knowing his notoriety for recklessness, to get him across the mountains. Greeley returned east to tell stories of his close encounter with death on this ride. Mark Twain, who worked at the *Tribune*, claimed he heard this story of Greeley's no less than 481 times!

In California, Greeley gave speeches in support of the Republicans, met with John C. Fremont, and observed fruit growing and mining. His overland journey of 1859 undoubtedly increased the visibility of the Republicans, the *Tribune*, and its editor.

X

Back East, the sectional crisis was entering its fateful final years. On October 19, 1859, readers of the *Tribune* learned that the "*The Insurrection,* so called, at Harper's Ferry, proves a verity." With a small group of followers, John Brown, a veteran of Bleeding Kansas, had attacked a federal arsenal at Harper's Ferry, Virginia. His plan—to launch a slave uprising in the South—ended in ignominious failure. "The whole affair seems the work of a madman," Greeley wrote, "but John Brown has so often looked death serenely in the face that what seems madness to others doubtless wore a different aspect to him." Similar to his reaction to the Dorr Rebellion in Rhode Island, Greeley objected to the use of violence to achieve political goals: "Believing that the way to Universal Emancipation lies not through insurrection, civil war and bloodshed, but through peace, discussion, and the quiet diffusion of sentiments of humanity and justice, we deeply regret this outbreak." Two days later, Greeley shifted the blame away from Brown and on to an aggressive slave power. Without Bloody Kansas, "Brown would have remained a quiet and industrious man, and would never have been heard of beyond the limits of his immediate neighborhood."

Brown stood accused of treason, was convicted by a Virginia jury, and was sentenced to hang. After his death, he became a martyr to many in the North. The *Tribune* contributed to his sanctification. "John Brown dead will live in millions of hearts," Greeley wrote, "—will be discussed around the homely hearth of Toil and dreamed of on the coach of Poverty and Trial." He further told his readers to be "reverently grateful for the privilege of living in a world rendered

At the 1860 Republican convention in Chicago, Greeley was instrumental in thwarting William H. Seward's presidential ambitions. (Courtesy of the Library of Congress)

noble by the daring of heroes, the suffering of martyrs—among whom let none doubt that History will accord an honored niche to Old John Brown."

Brown's raid on Harper's Ferry brought the sectional conflict to a dangerous precipice on the eve of the presidential election of 1860. The Republicans were cautiously optimistic, confident that the addition of Indiana, Illinois, or Pennsylvania would give them the presidency. Initially, Greeley supported former Whig Edward Bates of Missouri. Still alienated from Weed, Greeley was determined that the nomination not go to Seward. Indeed, many Republican strategists worried that Seward, even when he was looking like the front-runner, was too radical to be elected.

Illinois Republicans were pushing Lincoln for a dark-horse nomination. Lincoln came to New York and gave an address at Cooper Union on February 27. Greeley helped escort him to the platform. "No man ever before," Greeley said after the speech, "made such an impression on his first appeal to a New York audience."

Republicans from across the North and West gathered in Chicago for their national convention on May 8. Rebuffed by

New York Republicans, Greeley attended as a substitute delegate from Oregon. He was also a member of the platform committee, in which he later claimed that the homestead plank was "fixed exactly to my own liking." Greeley's major purpose at the convention seems to have been to defeat Seward. For this, he was later attacked by Weed in the Albany *Evening Journal* and Raymond's *New York Times*. When the balloting began, Greeley supported Bates for the nomination, but on the crucial third ballot switched to Lincoln.

After the Chicago convention, Greeley joined the Lincoln bandwagon. He claimed that there was "no truer, more faithful, more deserving Republican than Abraham Lincoln." In an editorial titled "Honest Old Abe," Greeley helped his readers learn more about the Republican standard-bearer. Spouting Republican ideology, Greeley extolled Lincoln's free-labor success story: "Thus hard work and plenty of it, the rugged experiences of aspiring poverty, the wild sports and rude games of a newly and thinly peopled forest region—the education born of the log-cabin, the rifle, the ax, and the plow, combined with the reflections of an original and vigorous mind, eager in the pursuit of knowledge, by every available means, and developing a character of equal resource and firmness—made him the man he has since proved himself." Greeley coauthored the *Political Textbook for 1860* and reprinted thousands of copies of Hinton Rowan Helper's *Impending Crisis of the South* (1860), a tract written by a North Carolinian showing the ill effects of slavery on the nonslaveholding whites of the South.

The presidential election of 1860 was a four-party race. Lincoln squared off against his nemesis Douglas, the nominee of Northern Democrats; John C. Breckinridge of the Southern Democrats; and John C. Bell of the Constitutional Union Party. In the October state elections, the Republicans won key victories in Pennsylvania, Indiana, and Ohio. The *Tribune* exulted: "BOYS, WE'VE GOT 'EM." With only a plurality of the popular vote, Lincoln captured 180 electoral votes and the presidency.

The year 1860 was truly a revolution. An antislavery political party had captured the North and elected a president. All eyes now turned to the South to see what the fruits of victory might bring.

Chapter Six

─────────○─────────

The Politics of Union
The Civil War

HORACE GREELEY WAS KNOWN FOR WEARING a white overcoat. During the Civil War, he carried a red-and-blue towel that essentially made his attire into a walking flag. Another story, similar in substance if not in precise sartorial detail, has Greeley carrying red, white, and blue cloth. The somewhat idiosyncratic attire of the editor of the *New York Tribune* serves as a useful metaphor for his public life from 1861 to 1865. Historians of the Civil War era often portray Greeley as "erratic." His support for the Lincoln administration fluctuated greatly. His vacillations supporting war and peace caused one biographer to assert that his peace overtures were the result of a "war psychosis." At one point in the war, a weary and confused President Lincoln asked, "What in the world is the matter with Uncle Horace?"

Greeley's public positions from 1861 to 1865 do show inconsistencies. At times, he joined Republican Radicals in advocating emancipation and the use of African American troops. Yet he was closely involved with efforts at a negotiated peace. Greeley's relationship with Lincoln during the war years was highly uneven, ranging from cooperation to vitriolic criticism. While these apparent inconsistencies are hard to refute, they are somewhat explainable. Like President Lincoln and other Northerners, Greeley was grappling with the myriad complexities of crushing the rebellion, restoring the Union, and addressing the fundamental cause of the war, slavery. It is also clear that there were some difficult times at the *Tribune*. After his visible role in dethroning William Henry Seward as the Republican standard-bearer at the 1860 Chicago convention, his place in the state and national party was unclear.

For our purposes, Greeley's "erratic" behavior during the Civil War might best be put in the larger context set forth in this book. The demands of wartime governance and the pressing issue of emancipation once again brought to the surface the ambiguities inherent in the politics of Whiggery, reform, and antislavery. It is clear that on the slavery question Greeley was more openly radical during the war years. Even as early as 1861, prominent New York conservative George Templeton Strong referred to Greeley along with Charles Sumner as the "Extreme Left" of the Republican Party. Yet the New York City Draft Riots of 1863, exposing the raw divisions of class, race, and ethnicity, drew out the more conservative elements in Greeley's nature. Simply stated, the Civil War raised in stark form the dilemmas of nineteenth-century liberalism.

I

The election of Abraham Lincoln in November 1860 confirmed the worst fears of Southern radicals. An antislavery Republican had won a majority of the popular vote in the North. If and when Republicans gained control of the presidency *and* Congress, what would stop them from openly attacking slavery? Southern secessionists, known as "fire-eaters" for their radicalism, seized on Lincoln's election as both a pretense and rationale for disunion.

Greeley recalled that Lincoln's election "was nowhere received with more general expressions of satisfaction than in South Carolina, whose ruling caste had . . . indicated their wish and hope that the election would have this issue." Shortly after the presidential election, the South Carolina legislature called for a convention to consider the question of secession. On December 20, 1860, the Palmetto State formally dissolved "the Union now subsisting between South Carolina and other States." Six other states of the Lower South—Alabama, Georgia, Mississippi, Florida, Louisiana, and Texas—soon followed suit. On February 4, 1861, representatives of these slave states met in Montgomery, Alabama, and formally established the Confederate States of America. The most momentous crisis in the history of the Union now faced the leaders in Washington.

As a leading Republican editor, Horace Greeley had a potentially important voice in how the North would respond to the secession crisis. For over a decade, Southern radicals had threatened antislavery Northerners with secession. During the 1850s, Greeley expressed ambivalence over the possibility of disunion. "If they choose to go," he wrote in 1856, "let them go." In the winter of 1860–1861, Greeley and the *Tribune* became associated with a view called "peaceable secession," the idea that the North should allow the disunionist South to depart in peace. "I had for forty years," Greeley recalled in his autobiography, "been listening with steadily diminishing patience, to Southern threats of Disunion." He had "become weary of this, and desirous of ending it." In December 1860, Greeley made several statements that could clearly be interpreted as sanctioning secession. "For our own part," he editorialized on December 17, "while we deny the right of slaveholders to hold slaves against the will of the latter, we cannot see how twenty millions of people can rightfully hold ten, or even five, in a detested union with them, by military force." Secession may have been disunion, but coercing the South to stay in the Union against their will would violate the principles of popular government. "We hold the right of self-government sacred," Greeley insisted, "even when invoked in behalf of those who deny it to others."

But at this time and place, Greeley felt, secession was wrong. In January, Greeley questioned whether secession was truly the choice of the Southern people or merely the decision of a small minority of "conspirators." "The South was *not* for Secession," Greeley recalled in his *Recollections of a Busy Life*. In *this particular case* then, the principle of self-determination did not apply. "It is anarchy even to admit the right of secession," Greeley tried to explain in an editorial from January 21: "It is to degrade our Union into a mere alliance, and insure its speedy ruin." These kinds of obfuscating comments confused Northerners, troubled President-elect Lincoln, and have

perplexed historians since. Greeley later claimed that he did not
have full control of the *Tribune*'s editorial policy that winter. He
insisted that the newspaper was pushed into a disunionist stance
by radical-leaning writers James S. Pike, Charles A. Dana, and Polish expatriate Adam Gurowski. After careful study, historian David
Potter attempted to clarify the *Tribune* editor's position: "Greeley
used disunion to defend the Union, offered secession to defeat the
secessionists, and agreed to an abstract proposition to forestall its
practical application."

After the Civil War, Greeley correctly remembered that the
"first breath of Disunion from the South fanned into vigorous life
the old spirit of compromise and cringing at the North." The sitting
president, Democrat James Buchanan, sat helplessly as the nation
crumbled around him. While he denied the right of a state to secede, he conceded that the federal government was powerless to
stop it. Congress met the crisis by turning to compromise efforts.

In December 1860, the House of Representatives created a
Committee of Thirty-Three composed of congressmen from each
state. This group proposed a constitutional amendment to protect
slavery in the states and advocated the enforcement of the Fugitive
Slave Law and a repeal of Northern personal liberties laws. The Senate likewise put together a Committee of Thirteen to resolve the secession crisis and proposed what became known as the Crittenden
Compromise, after Kentucky senator John J. Crittenden. The basis
of this proposal was extending the line of the original Missouri Compromise, 36 degrees 30 minutes north latitude, to the California
border. Slavery would be permitted south of the line, and territories
north of that line could enter the Union with or without slavery.

Perhaps the most ambitious effort to preserve peace was the
Washington Peace Conference that opened on February 4, 1861.
It included such old luminaries as former president John Tyler and
William Cabell Rives of Virginia, along with current Republican
leaders Senator William Pitt Fessenden of Maine and Salmon P.
Chase of Ohio. What became known as the "Old Gentleman's Con-
vention" proposed seven amendments to the Constitution that were
similar in essence to the Crittenden Compromise. Yet, by March

1861, sectional arguments had hardened to a point that made any real compromise impossible.

Despite the abortive failure of compromise efforts during the secession crisis, significant support for the Union existed on both sides of the Mason-Dixon Line. A strong unionist current ran through the South, and eight slave states still remained in the Union. Some Southerners remained committed to the Union and denied the principle of secession, while others admitted the right of the South to secede but opposed immediate secession. Another group of unionists wanted to cooperate with other slaveholding states.

Unionism was not an insignificant force during the secession winter. The popular vote in January for delegates to the Georgia convention was particularly close: 44,152 to 41,632. Secession was even rejected by conventions in Virginia and North Carolina. There was strong unionist sentiment in the North as well, especially among the mercantile community in New York. Conservative Republican Hamilton Fish and merchant Moses H. Grinnell backed compromise efforts. Greeley's old political associate Thurlow Weed also endorsed the idea of compromise.

During January and February 1861, Greeley opposed any compromise efforts. "My own controlling conviction from first to last was," Greeley later recalled, that "[t]here must, at all events, be no concession to Slavery." Greeley wrote Lincoln in January urging him to avoid any "nasty compromise" with the South. He told Senator Crittenden that the North would not capitulate to traitors. Greeley's reasoning echoed a belief he had expressed during the 1850s that "complicity in Slavery extension is guilt, which the Republicans must in no case incur." Greeley's opposition to compromise followed the majority Republican thinking during the secession crisis. Lincoln himself was adamant that Republicans not capitulate on the issue of slavery in the territories. "Entertain no proposition for a compromise in regard to the extension of slavery," he wrote an Illinois congressman. Greeley agreed with Lincoln that the government should remain operative and that any resistance would constitute treason.

Leading Republicans, including Greeley, Seward, and Lincoln, shared a faith in the latent power of Southern unionism to avoid war. Yet by April it became abundantly clear that they had overestimated the strength of unionism in the South. On April 12, Confederate forces in Charleston fired on Fort Sumter, which surrendered after forty hours of bombardment. Three days later, Lincoln called for seventy-five thousand troops to put down the "combinations" in seven states "too powerful to be suppressed by the ordinary course of judicial proceedings." The Civil War in America had begun.

II

Horace Greeley sat behind President Abraham Lincoln as he read his first inaugural address on March 4, 1861. We do not know how much Greeley was aware on this "bright, warm, still March day" that Lincoln's inauguration signaled a new epoch for himself and for the political life of the United States. A new Republican administration was taking the helm of statecraft, and in a little more than a month the nation would be at war. During the first few years of the Civil War, Greeley would have to negotiate his roles as *Tribune* editor and Republican politician on both the state and national levels. He associated strongly with the Radical faction in the Republican Party, but never established a consistent or friendly relationship with President Lincoln.

The beginning of Greeley's Civil War career was not auspicious. Already, factionalism within the New York Republican Party was rearing its ornery head. Seward, as Lincoln's choice for secretary of state, obviously held a position of power and influence within the administration. Greeley, along with fellow New York editor William Cullen Bryant, had opposed Seward's nomination at the 1860 Republican national convention in Chicago, so some New York Republicans were pushing Greeley for a cabinet position to counter the influence that Seward and Thurlow Weed would have with Lincoln. Greeley himself, however, was eying the Senate seat that had been vacated by Seward. But his old political ally and current nemesis Weed thwarted Greeley's quest for the Senate, gloating that he had paid "the *first* installment on a large debt to Mr. Greeley."

When Greeley met with Lincoln in Springfield, Illinois, on February 5 about appointments in New York, he felt the lingering animosity of Illinois Republicans from the 1858 Senate race. One hostile legislator, stung by former congressman Greeley's mileage crusade, suggested that a new Cabinet position be created for Greeley: a "secretary of the exterior," whose job it would be to watch the thermometer and report how cold it was outside. By early March, Greeley seems to have abandoned any political ambitions. "I was not made for a scramble for office," he wrote to a friend, "and I am not fit for it." "My business is to edit newspapers," Greeley wrote, "and I am good for that if anything."

Perhaps consoling himself after these political rejections, Greeley wanted the freedom to "denounce the whole administration should it take a course which seems inconsistent with principle and the public good." Yet in 1861 Greeley's career as newspaper editor was not faring much better. In late May, Greeley injured himself while trimming trees at his Chappaqua home. In his absence, Charles A. Dana took over editorial control. Aggravating matters in the summer of 1861 was an illness diagnosed as an "attack of brain fever" that took him away from the *Tribune* for six weeks.

By March 1862, Dana was forced out, most likely because of the train of radical journalists (including Karl Marx) he hired. Still, the *Tribune* remained a journalistic force. In late 1861, Lincoln wanted to make the *Tribune* a steadfast supporter of his administration: "Having [Greeley] firmly behind me will be as helpful to me as an army of one hundred thousand men." Even though Greeley had been critical of the administration, a private agreement that Greeley would support Lincoln in return for inside information was arranged. This worked for a short time. Gradually, Greeley grew impatient with Northern defeats and disappointed with the type of inside news fed to him from Lincoln's circle.

In the spring of 1861, anxious eyes looked to the Lincoln administration to end the rebellion. An initial wave of patriotic fervor spread across the North as young men enlisted, worried that the war would be over before they could achieve military glory. Even

Stephen A. Douglas, the standard-bearer of Northern Democrats in the election of 1860, traveled through Illinois rounding up support for the war. Yet Lincoln's effort to repress the rebellion was not fast enough for Greeley. "Instead of energy, vigor, promptness, daring, decision," he recalled about the first days of the war, "we had in our councils weakness, irresolution, hesitation, delay." Under the editorial leadership of Dana, the *Tribune* urged prompt action. Editorials titled "Forward to Richmond!" (a phrase apparently the product of a newspaper stringer) blazoned the pages of the newspaper.

With the public clamoring for action, Union general Irvin McDowell moved against a Confederate force stationed at Manassas Junction in Virginia. On July 21, 1861, McDowell hurled his forces against the Confederates. Expecting a quick and glorious victory, congressmen and other spectators organized picnics to watch the battle. Successfully dislodging the Confederates lying on the south bank of Bull Run, McDowell was surprised by a Confederate counterattack later in the afternoon. The Union retreat turned into a rout. Terrified picnickers fled with panicked Union troops.

Greeley's journalistic rivals in New York placed responsibility for the defeat at Bull Run on the *Tribune* promotion of war fever. The editor of the *New York Herald* called the *Tribune*'s staff a bunch of "ferocious Jacobins," a name harkening back to the excesses of the French Revolution.

Despondent about the Union defeat and smarting from the criticism, Greeley wrote Lincoln on July 29, 1861. Unfortunately, Greeley was suffering from both a fever and sleepless nights, so the letter had more than a little incoherency. On the one hand, Greeley urged an aggressive fight against the rebels, yet in the same letter he urged that Lincoln pursue peace with the Confederacy. "You are not considered a great man," Greeley wrote. John Hay, one of Lincoln's private secretaries, later called this "the most insane specimen of pusillanimity that I have ever read."

Throughout the rest of 1861 and 1862, Greeley vacillated in his faith in the Union cause and his views of Lincoln. Looking back with hindsight, he recalled that Lincoln had made the mistake of "underestimating the spirit and power of the Rebellion." In Greeley's opinion, Lincoln should have immediately held a kind of universal draft of all able-bodied Northern men. Greeley held Lincoln "most inapt" for the leadership of a people involved in desperate, agonizing war. His political leadership was no more than mediocre. Greeley was also critical of Lincoln's oversight of Northern military commanders: "If the incompetency of some Generals, the treachery of others, and the mean, despicable jealousies and low ambitions of still more, shall cause a further miscarriage of the National efforts, not only will the Administration be execrated, but the Nation will be ruined." In September 1863, Greeley queried Lincoln, "How many officers whose 'sympathies are with the South' have you today in important positions? How many whom you know to be drunkards are you allowing still to lead our heroes to sure destruction?"

Inexplicably, Greeley sounded optimistic at a point when Northern morale was at a low. After the devastating and humiliating defeat of Union forces at Fredericksburg in December 1862, Greeley urged his readers to "stand by the Government, and stand by ourselves, and traitors everywhere will yet be made to bite the dust."

By the end of 1861, it became clear that the military conduct of war was inseparable from Northern politics. After the military disappointment of Bull Run and impatient with what it saw as General George McClellan's feeble prosecution of the Union war effort, Congress created a Joint Committee on the Conduct of the War. The congressmen behind this effort were largely a group called the Radical Republicans. The Radicals not only urged a more vigorous prosecution of the war but also insisted that the war's aims include emancipation. Senator Charles Sumner of Massachusetts and Representative Thaddeus Stevens of Pennsylvania were the most vocal leaders of this group, which also included senators Benjamin Wade of Ohio and Zachariah Chandler of Michigan. Many of the wartime Radicals had been at the forefront of antislavery efforts before the Civil War. White House secretary John Hay dubbed them the "Jacobins."

For most of the Civil War, Horace Greeley sided with the Radical Republicans. According to one recent student of Civil War politics, "Greeley's importance to the radical Republican organization cannot be overstated." His alliance with the Radicals rested primarily on shared ideas regarding emancipation. At a January 1862 lecture at the Smithsonian Institution with a discomfited Lincoln in attendance, Greeley called for an end to slavery. By the spring and summer, Greeley became more vocal in his support of emancipation. In 1863, Greeley appeared at an antislavery meeting at Cooper Union in New York with abolitionist legend William Lloyd Garrison. Greeley also supported the Radicals in their attempt to oust Secretary of State Seward from the Cabinet in December 1862. And like many Radicals, Greeley was critical and suspicious of the Blair family in Missouri and Maryland.

Greeley shared with Radical Republicans an intense dislike of Democratic opponents of the war. Within the Democratic Party, a group of "War Democrats" played the role of a loyal opposition by generally supporting the prosecution of the war. Yet there was another faction, known as "Peace Democrats" (or, more insultingly, as "Copperheads"), who wanted to restore the Union and leave slavery untouched. As a Republican editor, Greeley often associated war resistance with the Democrats. He insisted that "no resistance to the draft has been made in any township or neighborhood that does not give large majorities for that sort of Democracy which is in affiliation with [Horatio] Seymour, [Clement] Vallandingham, Fernando Wood & Co." In a *Tribune* editorial from October 1862, Greeley warned that "their plan is to have the loyal States exhausted and wearied out by delays and disappointments, until the Administration shall be compelled to make a Disunion peace, which (they calculate) will throw the Republicans out of office, when they will come in, and, by a completed prostration of the country at the feet of the Slave Power, they expect to be able to patch up a reunion." Two years later, he maintained that Democrats were involved in "the great conspiracy against the Union."

III

Emancipation was the central political question in the Civil War North, shaping national and state politics and military strategy. It helped define the factions of the wartime Republican Party. The decision of the Lincoln administration to abolish slavery, codified in the Thirteenth Amendment (1865), was arguably the most important outcome of the Civil War. At the same time, thousands of slave men and women by individual actions during wartime hastened the destruction of slavery. "Wherever the Armies of the United States penetrate the dominions of Jeff. Davis," Greeley recognized, "the slaves leave the plantations of their masters and escape if they can to some region where they hope to enjoy liberty."

As we have seen, Horace Greeley was not among the original abolitionists of the 1830s who first challenged the morality and justice of slavery. As a Republican in the 1850s, he was more concerned with stopping the spread of slavery into the territories and standing up to the demands of the slave power. Yet during the Civil War, Greeley moved quickly and forcefully into the ranks of the Radical Republicans and became an important voice for black freedom.

In the politics of emancipation, Greeley is perhaps best known as the author of the "Prayer of Twenty Millions." In the summer of 1862, Greeley was frustrated that emancipation was not making more headway. He urged the president to execute the law to hasten emancipation by insisting that the generals needed to obey the Confiscation Acts passed by Congress, which allowed for the emancipation of slaves used to support the Confederate war effort. On August 19, 1862, Greeley wrote a letter to Lincoln reproaching him for moving slowly on slavery and urging him toward emancipation. The letter was printed in the *Tribune* on August 20 as the "Prayer of Twenty Millions."

Lincoln's response to Greeley, telegraphed to the *Tribune* office, has become one of the most quoted documents in tracing Lincoln's course toward the Emancipation Proclamation: "My paramount object *is* to save the Union, and *is not* either to save or to destroy slavery. . . . What I do about slavery, and the colored race, I do because I believe it helps to save the Union; and what I forbear, I forbear because I do *not* believe it would help to save the Union." Greeley's reply to Lincoln four days later evinces his support of government-sponsored emancipation: "That law—in strict accordance with the law of nations, of Nature, and of God—declares that every traitor now engaged in the infernal work of destroying our country has forfeited thereby all claim or color of right lawfully to hold human beings in slavery."

Even before Greeley's public prayer, Lincoln had made up his mind to issue an emancipation edict. After discussing his decision with the Cabinet, however, the president decided to wait for a military victory to announce it. He feared that without it, emancipation would appear as an act of desperation. After Union troops stopped a Confederate advance into Maryland at Antietam on September 17, Abraham Lincoln announced the proclamation on September 22, 1862.

Contrary to later popular belief, the Emancipation Proclamation did not abolish slavery in the United States. Legally, Lincoln freed the slaves only in areas under Confederate control. Slavery in the loyal states such as Maryland and Delaware and within Union-occupied Confederate territory remained untouched. For constitutional reasons, Lincoln justified emancipation as a military necessity. Still, the Emancipation Proclamation changed the nature of the conflict to a war not only to preserve the Union but also to end slavery.

Greeley was understandably elated at this strike against slavery. In an editorial on September 27, he explained that President Lincoln "has decreed that the 1st of January next shall shatter for ever the chains of Four Millions of human beings." Like many mid-nineteenth-century Americans, Greeley saw the proclamation in apocalyptic terms, calling it "one of those stupendous facts in human history which marks not only an era in the progress of the nation, but an epoch in the history of the world." Despite the proclamation's limitations, Greeley saw in it a new birth of freedom in America. "It is the beginning of the end of the Rebellion," the *Tribune* editorialized, "the beginning of the new life of the nation. GOD BLESS ABRAHAM LINCOLN!" The Emancipation Proclamation had transformed "a State sunk in the semi-barbarism of a medieval age to the light and civilization of the Nineteenth Christian Century."

Greeley elaborated on the meaning of emancipation in an editorial titled "Readjustment of Ideas." Putting the momentous event in context, the *Tribune* editor explained that a "sudden trial throws a nation so violently back upon itself, and demands such instant exertion of power to meet the uppermost emergency, that it is a long while before a State can see around the cause of its disaster, and so aim to surround and crush it." Thus, slavery was behind the Civil War, even though its centrality could not be seen immediately: "Therefore the great Providence of nations changed the mode of appeal, and has forced us by physical means to do what we would not yield as a moral concession."

A national epiphany was necessary to comprehend the magnitude of emancipation. Greeley cautiously defended the measure from charges that black freedom meant social equality. In responding to such fears, he maintained that "there is no provision in the document obliging James Brooks [author of a letter to the *Tribune*] to ask Mr. Frederick Douglass to breakfast, and fortunately for Mr. Douglass, there is no provision obliging him to accept the invitation should Mr. Brooks proffer it." For Greeley, the Emancipation Proclamation did not go far enough, for he supported black freedom everywhere, including the border states.

IV

Yet the race question could not be avoided. For four days in July 1863, urban riots shook New York to its foundations. The first draft in the history of the United States served as the immediate catalyst for the riots, but the underlying causes were economic problems, class resentments, and racial and ethnic tension that had been brewing since the 1850s. More than New York's compliance with the National Conscription Act was at issue. At stake were critical questions about the legitimacy of Republican governance, the aims of the Civil War, and the power of elite rule in New York City. The New York City draft riots forced Horace Greeley to face the possibility that the natural relations between labor and capital might not be harmonious but conflicted. At the same time, the riots confirmed his commitment to Republican emancipation and middle-class hegemony.

The Civil War had a significant, if uneven, impact on New York's economy. The once profitable cotton trade with the South had been disrupted, although the war did spur some new industries. For instance, pharmaceutical manufacturers such as Charles Pfizer and Edward Robinson Squibb raised production to meet wartime demands. The clothing industry also expanded. Brooks Brothers pioneered in the production of what soldiers would call "shoddy"—old rags poorly glued together that disintegrated with exposure to the elements. With the profits of the capitalists rising, the New York elite prospered. By 1863, 1 percent of New York's wealthiest residents earned 61 percent of the city's wealth. They patronized the new store of A. T. Stewart and a new Delmonico's restaurant at Fifth Avenue and 14th Street.

The Civil War did not bring similar fortunes to the great majority of New York's citizens, though. The workingmen and women of the city faced rampant inflation in the costs of food and rent. They suffered additionally from the excess of paper money, a scarcity of goods, and profiteering. Urban growth in the 1860s exacerbated these economic problems. New York's Sixth Ward, which had been represented briefly in Congress by Greeley, was now the most densely populated place on earth with 290,000 people per square mile.

Changing social relations of production were also transforming the landscape of Civil War New York. Conflict between labor and capital was growing particularly acute in industry. In the late antebellum era, artisans in consumer-finishing trades had witnessed a "bastardization" of production and a degradation of skilled labor. In the building and woodworking trades, workers were squaring off against aspiring subcontractors. The 1850s witnessed a rise in labor protest. Greeley participated in the Industrial Congress of 1850, which showed signs of division between middle-class reformers and working-class leaders. He brought to the labor reform of the 1850s a similar vision of reorganized production that lay behind his commitment to Association during the 1840s. According to historian Iver Bernstein, these ideas were "an attempt to reconcile artisan association with the presuppositions of competitive capitalism."

Since many of New York's industrialists were associated with the Republican Party, labor protest was likely to become political as well. By 1863, many labor and working-class leaders had targeted the nationalizing and centralizing policies of the Republicans. They argued that federal intervention in the economy was putting undue burdens on the city's poor. Moreover, they resented what they saw as Republican intervention in working-class lives. Industrial workers in shipbuilding, metal works, and machine manufacturing who congregated around New York's waterfront sought to protect the autonomy of working-class neighborhoods. The theme of unjust centralizing power that appealed to artisan craftsmen, industrial workers, and laborers would help draw them into the Democratic camp. All these factors helped shape the content and form of the draft riots.

As the Civil War intensified existing trends toward social stratification, class resentments, and labor strife, New York also developed a potent and dangerous strain of war resistance. Many merchants had had strong trading ties with the South that were broken by secession. The city also had a vibrant Democratic Party that naturally fostered opposition to a Republican administration. Democratic mayor Fernando Wood wanted the city to declare its independence. In 1862, Democrat Horatio Seymour became governor of New York with a strong belief in local control.

The advent of emancipation in late 1862 and early 1863 stiffened opposition to the war in New York. In February 1863, New York Democratic merchants created the Society for the Diffusion of Political Knowledge, which published tracts against the war and emancipation. A faction of Peace Democrats associated with Wood's Mozart Hall turned against the war when it became a war to end slavery. "Two years ago," one New Yorker wrote in 1862, "you could walk the entire length of Broadway without stepping on a snake," but now "New York swarms with Copperheads," a reference to antiwar Democrats.

Into this volatile setting came a national draft. Throughout the wartime North, Americans had to grapple with the meaning of an expanding national state. Conscription—the compulsory enrollment of men for military service—represented an unprecedented expansion of federal power. Greeley accepted the principle of a mandatory draft. Any state, he claimed, had the right to call for the service of its citizens "when imperiled by foreign invasion or domestic treason." Immigrants especially "ought peculiarly to realize that obligation and respond to its demands with conspicuous alacrity."

On March 3, 1863, Congress passed the First Conscription Act, which made all men from ages twenty to forty-five eligible for military service. A controversial provision of the draft law allowed a potential draftee to either hire a substitute to enlist for three years or pay a $300 commutation fee. This meant that wealthy New Yorkers could simply buy their sons out of the draft, heightening the identification of the Republican war with local elites. One city newspaper even advertised that "gentlemen will be furnished promptly with substitutes by forwarding their orders to the office of the Merchants, Bankers, and General Volunteer Association." The Conscription Act was also controversial in creating a large bureaucratic apparatus that included an army of provost marshals to enforce it.

Greeley supported the draft as a necessary and effective military option and approved the expansion of federal power that it represented. "The People," he claimed, "whose Constitution and Union are at stake, will tolerate in their rulers anything necessary to preserve them." Greeley even believed that the draft should be enforced by "the military power of the National Government" if necessary. Yet he was critical of particular measures like the one regarding substitutes. He also insisted on increasing the pay of the soldiers and connecting the draft to emancipation and the enlistment of black troops. Many New Yorkers, however, including Governor Seymour, protested the draft, claiming that a Republican draft set unfair quotas for Democratic New York City.

Implementation of the draft began in New York on Saturday, July 11. Anticipating trouble, federal authorities moved the site where names would be called to the edge of the city, the Ninth District Headquarters on Third Avenue and 47th Street. The names of the 1,236 draftees were published in newspapers on Sunday. Trouble began Monday morning when people were going to work. Crowds carrying placards reading "NO DRAFT" marched toward the provost marshal's office on Third Avenue, tearing up streetcar tracks along the way. The superintendent of police was beaten as he tried to intervene. The anger of the crowd was soon directed toward the symbols of wealthy Republicans, including Mayor George Opdyke's house. Over the next two days, the rage of the riot focused on New York's African American population. Blacks were dragged off streetcars—one was even lynched and his body burned. The crowds, composed of many Irish American workers fearful of labor competition and racial amalgamation, destroyed black homes and tore down the Colored Asylum.

In editorials after the riot, Greeley condemned the racial violence. "Resistance to the Draft," he argued, "was merely the occasion of the outbreak; absolute disloyalty and hatred to the Negro were the moving cause. It was not simply a riot but the commencement of a revolution, organized by the sympathizers in the North with the Southern Rebellion." He questioned the logic of the rioters: "What have the hanging and stamping to death of Negroes, what the sacking of private houses, what the pillaging of jewelry stores and of warehouses, to do with the draft?" On July 23, Greeley lauded the city's blacks for the "remarkable fortitude which they exhibited during the period of peril and alarm, and the still more extraordinary magnanimity which has characterized their conduct since." Greeley also stood with those Radicals who demanded that martial law be proclaimed in New York, urging "declaring that promptly, exercising it mercilessly, and maintaining it till the last vestige of treason is annihilated."

As a symbol of Republican antislavery, the *Tribune* was an inviting target to the draft rioters. To many New Yorkers, Greeley embodied the spirit of abolitionism that seemed to be dictating Republican war policy. The Democratic editor of the *New York Herald* insisted that Greeley "has attempted to break up the Union, and to put white men and black upon an equality in everything." In essence, he blamed Greeley for the Civil War, which "sacrifices thousands of valuable lives." "If abolitionists were to be hanged," the *Herald* suggested, "poor Greeley shall swing on the post of honor at the head or tail of the lot. We promise him that high honor."

On Monday, the first day of the riot, historian and biographer James Parton was walking in the late afternoon when he noticed "a strange looking gang of ruffians" chasing a black man on horseback and heading toward the *Tribune* building. The police dispersed the crowd, but Parton still went to warn the newspaper office. Another throng began to gather that night. The police protection that had been ordered to guard the *Tribune* had not materialized. Rioters threw rocks and broke windows. They overpowered five or six policemen and began to break down the doors and enter the building. When a pistol was fired, the crowd dispersed, but not before damage had been done. In the lower stories of the building, gas burners were twisted off, desks were overturned, and doors and windows battered in.

When advised to arm the office, Greeley refused and reportedly said, "All my life I have worked for the workingmen; if they would now burn my office and hang me, why, let them do it." Friend and fellow editor Theodore Tilton urged him not to go to the office that night, as he would be lynched. According to Parton, "all through the riots he seemed totally oblivious to the fact that he was in any personal danger." Even Molly, far away at their home in Chappaqua, prepared for the worst. She planned to blow up her house in case it was attacked. Ever the committed editor, Greeley managed to reassemble his staff after the assault, and they worked late that night to get out the paper in the morning.

The New York City draft riots lasted until Thursday evening. Close to six thousand federal troops, some drawn from the recent battle at Gettysburg, were keeping order in the streets of New York. It was the largest instance of civil disorder in American history up to that point, with at least 119 people killed.

Greeley's immediate response was to link the draft rioters to the larger opposition to the war, terming them "the Northern allies of the Virginia Army." In an editorial of July 16, 1863, he explained that the riot was "no sudden thing, no mere passionate resistance to the draft, but a concocted plan to begin by what should seem a riot an organized resistance to the Government which should compel it to end the war and accept any terms of peace that the Jeff. Davis Confederacy may condescend to grant." He attacked Democratic governor Seymour in particular as disloyal.

Greeley turned next to the Irish of New York. He explained first that when mobs "generally act solely from prejudice stimulated into headlong passion, and with no view but a distorted one, of ulterior consequences, the chances are that they will generally defeat whatever purposes they may really entertain." In this case, the Irish would suffer from their wanton attacks on the city's black population. Greeley insisted that "the principal effect of their barbarity has been to create in classes heretofore indifferent, or to some extent sharing the low prejudices of the base and lewd, a feeling of indignation at the diabolical atrocities to which these unoffending and helpless men, women and children have been subjected."

In his attack on the rioters, Greeley revealed a latent Whiggish distrust of democracy. Mobs were evidence that the people could be easily misled. "A mob is a great, many-handed and brainless beast," Greeley explained on July 21, "swollen by low instincts, and in spite of accidental and temporary chivalry, full of feline treachery, and no more to be trusted than the man of the menagerie trusts his best Bengal tiger." Greeley drew a distinction between mobs and genuine popular uprisings. Mobs were "those passionate demonstrations which indicate only an irrational discontent, a temporary anger, an unwholesome appetite for power, or a discreditable faith in the arts, low but subtle, of the demagogue." In contrast, a revolution "proposes to pass from one condition of things to another."

The various traumas of the Civil War, even to a noncombatant like Greeley, did not stop him from writing. In the midst of wartime, Greeley was approached by a Hartford publisher to write a history of the Civil War. From August 1863 to the spring of 1864, he worked on the book seven hours a day. Searching the libraries of New York for material, he was able to produce a chapter every three or four days. The fruit of his labor was *The American Conflict*. The first volume appeared on April 10, 1864, to coincide with the twenty-third birthday of the *Tribune*. The book sold 125,000 copies by 1867, adding to Greeley's personal financial prosperity. Within a few months of publication, he had earned $10,000 in royalties.

V

In 1864, the United States faced a wartime presidential election. Abraham Lincoln sought reelection, but was far from confident about his chances. The war ground on as generals Grant and Lee squared off in Virginia. Many Republicans, especially those Radicals who were impatient with the pace of emancipation, looked beyond Lincoln for their presidential candidate.

"Though I very heartily supported it when made," Greeley recalled in his autobiography, "I did not favor his re-nomination as President; for I wanted the War driven onward with vehemence, and this was not in his nature." Greeley's memory was correct, for during 1864 he supported various plans to nominate another Republican besides Lincoln. Along with William Cullen Bryant of the New York *Evening Post*, he wanted to delay the meeting of the Republican national convention.

In a broadside of February 24, 1864, a day after Greeley himself had called for another candidate, Senator Samuel C. Pomeroy of Kansas announced that Lincoln was not electable and proposed the nomination of current secretary of the treasury and Radical Salmon P. Chase. Yet Chase's proffer generated little interest and the short-lived "Chase boom" faded out.

Radicals in the party then turned to John C. Fremont, who had been the Republican presidential candidate in 1856. Fremont was popular with the antislavery wing of the Republican Party for his efforts to abolish slavery in Missouri before the Emancipation Proclamation. A "radical democracy" meeting took place in Cleveland on May 31, 1864. Greeley did not attend, but supported the movement along with such radical abolitionists as Frederick Douglass and Wendell Phillips.

Despite these abortive efforts, the Republicans nominated Lincoln for a second term at their national convention on June 8. Actually, Lincoln ran on a Union ticket with War Democrat Andrew Johnson as his running mate. Greeley disapproved of the vice presidential candidate, as he preferred a man with more solid antislavery convictions.

The Radicals did not give up hope. In September, a group including Greeley, Benjamin Butler, Henry Winter Davis, Theodore Tilton, and Parke Godwin planned a revolt against Lincoln's nomination. Angered by the president's veto of the Wade-Davis Bill (a more stringent plan for reconstructing the Southern states proposed in Congress), they sent out letters to Republican governors. Yet this movement also died out, especially after George McClellan was nominated by the Democrats and General William Tecumseh Sherman captured Atlanta on September 3.

After September, Greeley threw his support to Lincoln. "We MUST reelect him," he wrote in a *Tribune* editorial, "and God helping us, we WILL." Greeley raised money for Lincoln's re-election and gave speeches on his behalf. He acknowledged that the Union Party platform "affirms that as Slavery was the cause and now constitutes the strength of the Rebellion, it ought, in the interest of public tranquility and safety, to be abolished and prohibited." Greeley also continued to support the use of African American troops to fight for the Union.

Despite his own pessimism, Lincoln defeated McClellan in the November election. "ABRAHAM LINCOLN IS RE-ELECTED PRESIDENT," proclaimed the *Tribune*: "He is the choice of the American People by a preponderance which must disconcert and baffle the conspirators for North-Western and other Rebel-parasite Confederacies."

VI

In one of the many puzzles of Civil War history, Horace Greeley was associated with several peace efforts. In January 1863, he was in contact with French minister Henri Mercier about brokering a peace settlement. At the same time, he paradoxically insisted that any formal peace negotiations be undertaken by officials of the government. Secretary of State William H. Seward—and no longer an associate of Greeley's—rejected Mercier's offer of arbitration. Greeley was also in correspondence with Copperhead leader Clement L. Vallandingham of Ohio. Abolitionists such as Theodore Tilton, editor of the *Independent*, were angered by these overtures.

On July 7, 1864, Greeley pleaded with Lincoln that "our bleeding, bankrupt, almost dying country also longs for peace,—shudders at the prospect of fresh conscriptions, of further wholesale devastations, and of new rivers of human blood." Similarly, New York diarist George Templeton Strong expressed his belief that nine-tenths of all Americans were "anxious for peace—peace on almost any terms—and utterly sick of human slaughter and devastation." Greeley's blueprint for peace included a restoration of Union, the abolition of slavery, complete amnesty, and compensation to the South for emancipation.

How can the peace-seeking Greeley be reconciled with the Radical sympathizer Greeley who pushed Lincoln on emancipation and supported the Radical approach to Reconstruction? Part of the explanation might lie in a strain of pacifism that ran throughout Greeley's career. Greeley's vacillating relationship with Lincoln might also have been a factor. Finally, it seems obvious that the demands of his public life during the Civil War created great stress.

The Niagara Peace Conference of 1864 marked Greeley's greatest involvement with peace efforts. One historian calls him the "leading participant in the peace negotiations at Niagara Falls." Confederate president Jefferson Davis, still smarting from a Union cavalry raid into Richmond to free Northern prisoners, sent emissaries into Canada to foment more active resistance to the war in the North. Into this situation entered former Young America Democrat George N. Sanders and William Cornell "Colorado" Jewett, an adventurer with an unscrupulous reputation. Jewett told Greeley that "two ambassadors of Davis & Co. are now in Canada, with full and complete powers for peace." Greeley referred the matter to Lincoln, who then sent the editor to Niagara Falls to meet with these Confederates upon the conditions of a restoration of the Union and the abolition of slavery.

Greeley was reluctant to go, for he did not want to be involved with negotiations that had little chance of success. He nonetheless arrived in Niagara on July 17 and made contact with the commissioners. Before any meaningful discussions took place, Greeley apparently did not accurately convey Lincoln's terms. He also wanted to provide these men safe conduct to Washington. When Lincoln demanded an unconditional surrender and discovered that the emissaries were not official representatives, he cut off negotiations.

Greeley was criticized for his involvement in this abortive meeting. Charles Francis Adams, the U.S. ambassador to England, dubbed it a "fiasco." Yet even after Lincoln's reelection, Greeley continued to demonstrate an interest in a negotiated peace.

VII

By the spring of 1865, a Union victory was in the air. The Confederacy was rapidly collapsing on all fronts. After capturing Richmond, Ulysses S. Grant's Army of the Potomac continued to pursue the remains of Robert E. Lee's Army of Northern Virginia. Meanwhile, Sherman marched north through the Carolinas, cutting off any Southern avenue of retreat. By April, Lee was cornered in southern Virginia. Surrounded, exhausted, and defeated, Lee surrendered his army on April 9. The news of the final end of the Civil War reached the *Tribune* late that evening. Almost immediately, Greeley called for a general amnesty. Reflecting a pacific spirit he had not lost, he pleaded against "passions at this moment to be fierce and intolerant."

On the night of April 14, 1865, President Lincoln indulged in one of his favorite pastimes—the theater. He went to Ford's Theatre in Washington to see *Our American Cousin*, starring Laura Keene. During the play, he was shot by Southern sympathizer John Wilkes Booth. Lincoln died the next morning.

"When I last saw him, a few weeks before his death," Greeley recalled, "I was struck by his haggard, care-fraught face, so different from the sunny, gladsome countenance he first brought from Illinois. I felt that his life hung by so slender a thread that any new access of trouble or excess of effort might suddenly close his career." After his death, the *Tribune* editor came to his defense, praising his character and his transformation into a worldwide symbol of freedom. "Few graves will be more extensively, persistently visited, or bedewed with the tears of a people's prouder, fonder affection, than that of Abraham Lincoln."

In the late spring of 1865, Greeley and the nation turned their eyes to the vexing question of reconstructing the Union. Even less clear was the shape of post–Civil War America. Emancipation and the transformation of Northern government and society had created a new world in urban New York. There were new, more pressing questions about citizenship, democracy, and the relationship between labor and capital that would demand his attention. The years after the Civil War would constitute the last, but not the least eventful, chapter of Greeley's public life.

Chapter Seven

The Politics of Reconstruction

ON JULY 13, 1872, LEADING NATIONAL DEMOCRATS journeyed to Chappaqua, New York, to see Horace Greeley. While some came by the early morning train, most arrived by a special express "for the stoppage of which at Chappaqua the authorities of the road had previously arranged." Upon their arrival, Greeley welcomed each of his guests cordially and then invited them to take a drink. With Greeley's reputation as a temperance advocate, the visitors were understandably a bit confused. Nonetheless, they followed him through some woods to a hillside. When they reached the largest of the Chappaqua springs, "cups of cold water were profusely ladled to the intense amusement of the Southern delegates, many of whom declared themselves unaccustomed to taking water so freely without some little dilution." Around 2:00 p.m. that afternoon, a luncheon hosted by one of Greeley's daughters was served to the guests. An infirm Molly Greeley "was also lifted from her bed, and taken in a carriage to a grove, where she was able to remain for nearly an hour."

According to the report in the *Tribune*, "every state in the Union was represented by prominent Democrats." The list was indeed impressive and—considering Greeley's lifetime of politics and reform—unusual. From the South came former postmaster general of the Confederacy John H. Regan of Texas, Charleston *Courier* editor Thomas Y. Simons, and Albert Strassburger, president of the Montgomery, Alabama, Board of Trade. From the Old

Northwest came a former governor of Wisconsin and the son of Democrat-turned-Republican Lyman Trumbull of Illinois. Also at Chappaqua that afternoon was a young editor from the San Francisco *Post*, Henry George, who would later follow Greeley's legacy of land reform. A year earlier, George had published *Our Land and Land Policy*, which set forth a single-tax theory that he would later elaborate upon in *Progress and Poverty* (1879).

After lunch, Greeley mounted a chair to speak. "My friends," he began, "we have met in a merely social gathering, for no other purpose than to foster the good feeling and harmony that have sprung up between different parties, from widely separated sections of the Union." Greeley then said a few words "on the subject of my farm," a topic that "certainly need excite no apprehensions on the part of my political friends."

The *Tribune* editor explained that he and his wife had wanted a home in the country to provide a healthier environment for their children. "My wife's wants were few and simple," Greeley recalled—a spring with running water and an evergreen shade. They began with forty acres, on which they planned to build a house. Farming was hard. There were times Greeley did not think they would make it. In fact, he admitted to his visitors that he had not made much money. Yet his real purpose was not to make money, but to live closer to nature.

Echoes of Henry David Thoreau, a former correspondent of Greeley's, were audible in his speech. "I have an affection for my trees," Greeley explained, "and I do not put down to destroy, but to build up. Where I find dead or worthless trees hindering the growth of better and nobler trees I cut them down to make room for a nobler growth, and I trim off the lower pendant branches of the trees because I find that half the woods destroyed by fire have been lost by the thick condition of these lower limbs, which gives the fire fuel and headway." Greeley acknowledged his limitations as an agriculturalist: "Bad farmers make their blunders and go bullheaded right along. Now I have made blunders—new ones—but I never kept making old ones." He closed his pastoral oration with an invitation to his guests to return again someday.

The Chappaqua reception of 1872 raises several questions. Why were Southerners and Democrats—Greeley's adversaries for decades—coming in droves to visit the editor of the *New York Tribune*? And why would he entertain them with a lecture about horticulture?

The first question is easy to answer. Horace Greeley had received the endorsement of the Democratic Party for the presidential election of 1872, and party leaders were coming to Chappaqua to inform him of his nomination. A month earlier, he had been nominated by the Liberal Republicans, a group that had bolted from the regular Republican Party that stood behind President Ulysses S. Grant. However, the second question is more difficult to answer. Perhaps Greeley was consciously or unconsciously following a tradition deeply ingrained in nineteenth-century American culture. Perhaps farming served as a metaphor for his vision of national leadership. Greeley wanted his listeners to know that, unlike the sitting president, he himself was not seeking the White House for personal gain. Unlike Grant, he would get rid of "dead and worthless" officeholders through civil service reform. Like a careful horticulturalist, a President Greeley would keep the nation safe from another conflagration.

Greeley's presidential candidacy of 1872 was his last public act—he died shortly after the election. His participation in the abortive Liberal Republican revolt was not, in fact, a fitting end to his career as an editor, politician, and reformer. Rather, it tends to substantiate the adage that politics makes for strange bedfellows. A staunch protectionist, Greeley was allied with a movement consisting primarily of free traders. A leading Republican, he was endorsed by the Democratic Party.

For Greeley, the postwar era was the final chapter in his engagement with the two issues that defined his public career: the slavery controversy and the rise of industrial capitalism. The Civil War had created a new world in the North as well as the South. Like many Americans, Greeley would find that his ideological and political compasses would prove inadequate guides in negotiating the postwar world. The problems of Reconstruction magnified the ambivalence that Greeley had displayed in the pre–Civil War era. His belief in and desire for harmony proved much more problematic in facing the challenges of sectional and class reconciliation.

I

From 1865 to 1877, Americans were preoccupied with Reconstruction. The political, social, and economic challenges were enormous. The Civil War had shattered the foundations of the Southern social order, forcing whites and blacks to find new forms of race and labor relations.

The North had to secure the fruits of its victory while reintegrating the former states of the Confederacy into the Union. For most Northerners, the most immediate and minimum conditions were the abolition of slavery and the repudiation of secession. Greeley argued that the results of the Civil War had nullified the principle of slavery. Now, he declared, "this is to be a land of only free people."

In 1865, Reconstruction was in the hands of President Andrew Johnson. A former Democrat and Tennessee yeoman, Johnson was more eager to humiliate the former slaveholding aristocracy than to punish the South. Even though he favored a speedy and easy restoration of the Southern states without black suffrage, Johnson's moderate demands for Reconstruction were rebuffed by the South. Beginning in December 1865 and early 1866, Congress took over the task of Reconstruction. The Fourteenth Amendment, which essentially granted citizenship to former male slaves, was the centerpiece of congressional Reconstruction. Conflict between Johnson and Congress increased when Southern Democrats rejected the new amendment.

In 1867, Congress passed a new, more stringent plan of Reconstruction. The Military Reconstruction Acts divided ten former states of the Confederacy (Tennessee had been readmitted into the Union after ratifying the Fourteenth Amendment) into five military districts, allowed for the disfranchisement of whites, and mandated black suffrage for readmission into the Union. Radical Reconstruction culminated with the Fifteenth Amendment, which prohibited the states from denying the right to vote on the grounds of race or previous condition of servitude.

At least until 1870, Greeley was fairly consistent in his approach to Reconstruction. In a speech delivered in May 1866, he insisted that the Civil War had destroyed the idea of state sovereignty and enshrined the principle that "we are a nation." His plan for Reconstruction was summarized in a phrase that often appeared in the *Tribune*: "Universal Amnesty—Impartial Suffrage." Greeley maintained that equal rights should be "the corner-stone of a true, beneficent reconstruction." "If we shall close this long controversy with the negro still a serf," Greeley wrote to a friend in 1866, "we shall be a beaten bankrupt party, and shall have richly deserved our fate." African Americans deserved basic civil rights, he insisted: "There is no other land but ours on earth where a freeman, simply because of his color, is deprived of the essential rights of a freeman where everybody enjoys them." By supporting full civil liberties to the freedmen, Greeley aligned himself with the Radical Republicans in Congress.

Joining the ranks of the Radicals, Greeley soon parted ways with President Johnson. In early 1866, the president vetoed the Freedmen's Bureau bill and a civil rights bill passed by Congress. Greeley spoke out against Johnson's vetoes, which were promptly overturned by more than a two-thirds majority in Congress. In May 1866, one member of the *Tribune* staff wrote that the newspaper "has taken a bitter stand against Johnson, and we can't afford to see any good in him or his policy."

Greeley tried to reconcile Congress and Johnson in September 1866. Ever seeking accord, he suggested that three Northerners and three Southerners be invited to the White House, who "by free and friendly conference and discussion, should earnestly endeavor to find a common ground whereon the North and the South should not merely be reconciled, but made evermore fraternal and harmonious." After this and other attempts, however, Greeley concluded that President Johnson "*did not want* harmony with Congress, that he had already made up his mind to break with the party which had elected him, and seek a further lease of power through the favor

and support of its implacable enemies." Greeley claimed that Johnson was abandoning the freedmen for the sake of Southern whites.
Johnson returned the animosity. When Greeley was proposed for
a position in the Cabinet as postmaster general, Johnson objected
to the man whose "goodness of heart" had produced an "infirmity
of mind."

Greeley and the Radicals in Congress shared a commitment
to black freedom and civil equality but parted on the degree of
harshness that should be taken toward the South. This issue was
vividly brought to the fore with Greeley's assistance in securing a
pardon for Confederate president Jefferson Davis, one of the most
controversial acts of his public career. In the immediate aftermath
of the war and Lincoln's assassination, Greeley had joined others
in calling for Davis to be tried for treason, but during the next few
years, he gradually withdrew from this demand. Perhaps Greeley
was swayed by a letter from Davis's wife Varina: "You are powerful
with our party. Can you not restore us, dear Mr. Greeley, to our
little ones?"

More importantly, Greeley had firm grounds for urging a pardon. "The government had absolutely no excuse," Greeley explained
in an editorial, "for the long imprisonment of Jefferson Davis, and
its refusal to either release or try him." Moreover, he argued that
amnesty would be a clear gesture on behalf of sectional reconciliation. Greeley made known his desire to help Davis through a
lawyer. On May 13, 1867, Greeley met in the chambers of Judge
John C. Underwood in Richmond and cosigned a bail bond of
$100,000 to free Davis from federal prison after two years. Other
signers included abolitionist Gerrit Smith, railroad magnate Cornelius Vanderbilt, and former Virginia Whig and Unionist John
Minor Botts. According to the Richmond *Whig*, the posting of
Davis's bond was "accompanied and embellished by circumstances
of courtesy and cordial generosity from Northern and Republican
gentlemen of distinction and influence, which will go far to commend them to the grateful consideration of the South."

Greeley received a great deal of criticism for his role in the
pardon of Jefferson Davis. "I seem only to reap abuse," he wrote
afterward. Abolitionist and reformer Wendell Phillips criticized

Greeley for what he saw as his sycophantic approach to Davis. Editor E. L. Godkin of the *Nation* termed Greeley's action "simply detestable." The Davis pardon clearly hurt the sales of his second volume of *The American Conflict*. Thirty members of the Republican Union League Club of New York petitioned to expel Greeley from membership. Greeley chastised his opponents in an editorial published on May 29, 1867, insisting, "Those who are waiting for some defense, explanation, or apology from me, will wait for ever." After this, the majority of Union Leaguers decided not to expel him.

Meanwhile, the growing breach between the president and Congress led to Johnson's impeachment. In 1866, Greeley had rejected calls for impeachment on the grounds that it would throw the nation into convulsions and make Johnson a martyr. But the situation only worsened over the course of the year. On August 12, 1867, the president suspended Edwin M. Stanton from the War Department. Clearly, Johnson wanted men of similar views to execute and administer Reconstruction policy, but Stanton's dismissal and ultimate suspension angered Congressional Radicals. The *Tribune* editor in particular attacked Johnson for his failure to support General Philip Sheridan in his role as military commander of Texas and Louisiana. "Never was there a military ruler," Greeley claimed, "with so much reason to use force who has used so little."

The House of Representatives voted to impeach Andrew Johnson on February 24, 1868. The next day, the *Tribune* endorsed impeachment: "The President has been so reckless with his high trust he has so often dared Congress, as it were, to visit him with this penalty, that a hundred acts may be found in his administration coming within the constitutional meaning of 'high crimes and misdemeanors.'" In March, the *Tribune* claimed that "the consolidation of the Republican party in the House upon the impeachment resolution is fully paralleled by the consolidation of the newspapers, State Conventions, Legislatures, and political meetings all over the loyal States." It should be pointed out that the *Tribune*'s position against Johnson was largely directed by managing editor John Russell Young. Greeley supported this editorial policy, even while he was away on a speaking tour.

Greeley and the *Tribune* justified impeachment on several grounds. The editor argued that Johnson was out of touch with the American people. "The whole course of his opposition to the will of the people is a singular combination of stubbornness and insincerity," Greeley wrote in 1867. The president was "utterly blind to the events of the day and alienated from the spirit and purposes of his country."

Greeley also argued that Johnson's actions were illegal and unconstitutional and hence justified impeachment. The president had first usurped the function of Reconstruction from Congress. Johnson's actions during Reconstruction, in Greeley's eyes, signified a decline into tyranny. "Allow the Executive absolute power of removal and appointment," the *Tribune* editorialized, "and he may himself become in fact the Secretary of State, the Secretary of the Treasury, the Secretary of War. He may remove statesmen and appoint his creatures in their places. In theory such unlimited power as this absorbs all the departments of State in one, and makes the Cabinet an oligarchy, the President a tyranny." Johnson was compared to a tyrant, for he had used his power "to thwart the will of the people."

Finally, Greeley and the *Tribune* stressed that Johnson's actions as president were destructive to Reconstruction. "The President was bent on doing his wicked worst," an editorial read, "to baffle, evade, nullify, and defeat, the Reconstruction acts." His words and behaviors, another editorial stated, "[were] inspired with a passion of new resistance a Rebellion that was prostrate at our feet. The fruit of his policy was riot, and murder, and massacre; fresh hatred between the South and North; the long and costly delay of Reconstruction." On May 15, the *Tribune* warned that acquitting Johnson of impeachment would give the spirit of rebellion a new life in the South. When Johnson was acquitted on May 26, 1868, Greeley launched a bitter assault on the presiding judge, Supreme Court Justice Salmon P. Chase.

Throughout the 1860s, Greeley was consistent in his support for giving freed black men the right to vote. In 1866, he stated that the most important question about the postwar settlement was

"Manhood Suffrage." African Americans were entitled to vote for several reasons. First, they gained this privilege through military service to the Union during the war. Second, African American suffrage would bring valuable tangible results. "Enfranchise the Blacks," Greeley explained, "and further rebellions at the South are impossible." Third, and perhaps most important, was principle. Greeley supported black suffrage on the "the higher ground that they are MEN—citizens—loyal Americans." Southerners who opposed black suffrage pointed out that a number of Northern states did not extend the right to vote to African Americans, and Greeley admitted that it was "disgracefully true" that Republicans had not supported black suffrage in the Northern states.

Greeley elaborated on his views of black suffrage and civil rights in a speech delivered to a public meeting at the African Church in Richmond, Virginia, in 1867. He began by asking rhetorically "whether the time has not fully come when all the differences, all the heart-burnings, all the feuds and the hatreds which necessarily grew up in the midst of our great struggle, should be abandoned forever." The *Tribune* editor then offered some explanations for the failure of sectional and racial reconciliation. Unfortunately, he said, the fact that Lincoln's assassins were Southern sympathizers "tended to give an exceedingly malign aspect to that general calamity."

He next directed his ire at Southern whites. By passing the Black Codes, Greeley declared, Southern state legislatures were revealing the persistence of their racial prejudice. Greeley believed that these laws were "one of the chief obstacles, and . . . one of the still remaining impediments, to an early and genuine reconstruction of the Union." Greeley also recognized that the 1866 riots in Memphis and New Orleans convinced many Northerners that "no reconstruction would be real and enduring which did not include guaranties for the rights of the colored people of the South." Finally, Southern whites should also be appreciative of how former slaves acted during the Civil War.

Greeley continued his speech, turning to the subject of the suffrage and addressing the Southern conservative objection that blacks should not vote because they believed them to be ignorant. "But so long as ignorance or degradation is no bar to citizenship as to white men," Greeley retorted to this excuse, "I protest against making it a bar to suffrage on the part of black men, who have excuses for ignorance which white men have not." Greeley then spelled out to his audience the Radical Republican logic of equal rights: "I insist, then, in the name of justice and humanity, in the name of our country, and of every righteous interest and section of that country, that the rights of all the American people—native or naturalized, born such or made such—shall be guaranteed in the State constitution first, and in the Federal Constitution as soon as possible,—that we make it a fundamental condition of America law and policy, that every citizen shall have, in the eye of the law, every right of every other citizen."

In facing the challenge of Reconstruction, Greeley continued to rely on the precepts of classical liberalism. He shared a reluctance strong in the mid-nineteenth century in using the power of the state to mandate civil rights. In several editorials, Greeley voiced his belief that African Americans should not get what we today would call preferential treatment. He once criticized Wendell Phillips for wanting only black candidates for office. "This seems to us," Greeley responded, "akin to the Democratic error which would *exclude* men from office for that identical reason." In a July 1867 editorial titled "A Black Man's Party in the South," Greeley explained further: "These men in the South who are working to establish a black man's party are the enemies of this principle of equality, and if they carry out their plans they will strike Republicanism a blow far heavier than the Democracy can deal."

The premises of laissez-faire and limited government also surfaced in Greeley's comments on confiscation. During the early years of Reconstruction, Radical Republicans such as Thaddeus Stevens argued that the former plantations in the defeated South should be confiscated from their owners, divided into small farming plots, and distributed among those who had been freed. As early as 1865, former slaves in the South Carolina low country had insisted that true freedom could exist only with independent landownership. Here blacks were expressing republican notions of freedom that had informed Anglo-American thought since the Revolution.

Like many Republicans, Greeley approached the possibility of confiscation reluctantly. Avoiding the question of its essential justice, he argued that confiscation was impractical. It "will be found a very tedious process that years would be required to consummate." It would, moreover, paralyze agriculture. Altogether, Greeley wrote, "we shall realize that inevitable evils of confiscation are too great to justify an experiment of this character." Not surprisingly, Greeley suggested a homestead measure for the freedmen—selling public lands to Southern farmers at $10 for 160 acres. His arguments had been rehearsed decades before: "Become land-owners, all of you, so soon as you may," he told an African American audience. "Own something which you can call a home. It will give you a deeper feeling of independence and of self-respect, and do not wait to obtain a home by confiscation."

The scope of Republican Reconstruction extended beyond the boundaries of race and the South. By greatly accelerating the process of industrialization and revolutionizing American finance, the Civil War had given rise to new and pressing economic problems. During Reconstruction, Greeley revealed his continuing reliance on Whig liberal economic theory. He accepted the principle of government intervention in the economy and even foresaw the regulation of tenements, conditions in coal mines, and railroad rates. After the war, Greeley remained a staunch advocate of tariffs. Protection, he believed, would allow for the development of American industry and benefit the farmer by providing a market for agricultural products. The tariff would also help labor, Greeley insisted, reflecting his Whiggish assumption of a harmonious economy of labor, industry, and agriculture.

The *Tribune* editor was quick to attack free trade, a cause that drew an increasing number of adherents in the postwar era. He singled out David Ames Wells, special commissioner of the revenue from 1866 to 1869, accusing him personally as "bought and paid for by the foreign interest." Greeley also attacked future Greenbacker and Populist Ignatius Donnelly as "a false, selfish, unworthy man" who "cares nothing for the Republican party except as it ministers to his own aggrandizement."

Questions of finance were particularly contested during Reconstruction. Greeley opposed a repudiation of the national debt acquired during the Civil War, insisting on "a scrupulous fidelity to the Nation's most sacred engagements, made when she hung between life and death." Greeley also called for the elimination of "greenbacks" (paper currency issued during the Civil War) and the resumption of specie payments. He objected to paying the Five-Twenty Bonds in greenbacks, arguing that these and other "indirect paths" that were being suggested "would shame any swindler who ever uttered counterfeit money or passed off bogus checks." In November 1866, he wrote Schuyler Colfax urging Congress to pass some "decisive Retrenchment measures."

In the foreign affairs of Reconstruction, Greeley again followed the political principles he had developed during the antebellum decades. He did not share in the expansionist fervor following the Civil War. Specifically, he opposed the acquisition of Russian Alaska. During the spring of 1867, the Senate was discussing a treaty that called for the purchase of Alaska for $7 million. "On paper it is a wonderful country," Greeley wrote; "on ice it is what is generally called a big thing." Considering their contentious political past, Greeley was not likely to support any plan of Secretary of State William H. Seward's. Suggesting that Alaska was a "Quixotic land hunt," Greeley argued that the purchase would require excessive taxation. Additionally, it might prove to be a diplomatic affront to Great Britain.

In 1868, a revolution against Spanish rule broke out in Cuba. The revolutionaries declared Cuba a republic in April 1869. Greeley became vice president of the Cuban Aid Society, which sent supplies, urged U.S. recognition, and supported the emancipation of slaves. His penchant for republican revolutions for self-rule also made Greeley sympathetic to the Fenians, an Anglo-American group of Irish nationalists during the 1860s fighting for an independent Ireland. He supported the Irish fight for freedom, arguing that every race had "natural, inalienable rights." In general, the *Tribune* was sympathetic toward the Fenians.

II

The aftermath of the Civil War brought changes to Greeley's family and his newspaper. Sadly, his personal life offered little comfort. Greeley's father Zaccheus was still living, though disabled. Horace and his wife Molly drifted further apart. As she became increasingly sick, Greeley confessed she "needs more attention than I am able to give her." As her physical and mental health deteriorated, it became more difficult to secure household help that could tolerate Molly. The Greeley daughters, Ida and Gabrielle, were brought home from school to help their mother.

Meanwhile, New York's world of print culture continued to expand. By 1870, there were 150 newspapers in the city. Technological changes allowed the production of up to twenty thousand copies per hour. At the *Tribune*, Whitelaw Reid—former war reporter from the Cincinnati *Gazette*—became editor in 1868 and served as Greeley's second in command. Greeley still was known for his difficult personality. As editor, he was often irritable and sometimes explosive. He continued to have adversarial relationships with other New York editors, including Manton Marble and James Bennett. Mark Twain, who was hired as foreign correspondent for the *Tribune* in June 1867, related the story of Greeley shaving with a dull razor, punctuating a monologue with "Damn the damned razor, and the damned outcast who made it." While still editing the *Tribune*, Greeley was a frequent contributor to the *Independent* and other newspapers.

III

New York manifested in sharp and exaggerated form the social changes accelerated by the Civil War. The progress of industrial capitalism and urban growth created a more stratified social order with marked class and ethnic conflict. The economic revolution raised new challenges in the ongoing nineteenth-century attempt to reconcile capitalism and democracy. As an editor and reformer, Horace Greeley was forced to respond to these new conditions. He increasingly discovered the growing incongruity between his long-cherished beliefs and the challenges of a new order.

While the nation was embroiled in Reconstruction, New Yorkers—as usual—were going about their own business. William Marcy Tweed, commissioner of the Department of Public Works,

was modernizing New York and building a political machine, constructing roads, sewers, water pipes, and gas lines while lining his
own pockets. Alfred Ely Beach was thinking about a way to move
large numbers of people from uptown residential areas to work
downtown. In 1868, he devised a plan to move cars underground
through tunnels by compressed-air shafts. When—or if—these
subway commuters arrived at work, they would see a transformed
downtown landscape. Hundreds of private banks, trust companies,
and life insurance firms filled the financial district after the Civil
War. Anticipating the future, New Yorkers built upward. The
advent of the elevator allowed buildings to grow as high as eight
stories. When they were not working, city residents enjoyed an
increasing variety of entertainments, including skating and bicycle
riding in Central Park. By 1867, there were more than one hundred
baseball clubs in Manhattan and Brooklyn.

   After the Civil War, a wave of economic prosperity transformed
New York. When Walt Whitman walked around the city in the fall
of 1870, he was struck by the "hurrying, feverish, electric crowds
of men." He noted the splendor and glitter, but also the vulgarity
and capriciousness, that accompanied major transformations in the
economy. The balance of wealth in New York had shifted from merchants to manufacturers and financiers. In 1870, New York controlled 24 percent of all banking resources in the nation. Railroads
doubled their mileage between 1865 and 1873, raising the fortunes
of such New Yorkers as Cornelius Vanderbilt and Jay Gould. In the
United States, the number of factories almost doubled between
1859 and 1869; in Manhattan between 1860 and 1870, the total
grew from 4,375 to 7,624. Moreover, the rapid mechanization of
production tripled the number of factory workers.

   A New York bourgeoisie emerged in the era of the Civil War—a
class of merchants, industrialists, bankers, real estate developers,
and professionals. They formed social networks, created new institutions, and articulated a coherent worldview that reflected their
developing class consciousness. As newly self-defined property
owners, they sought urban reform through such organizations as
the Union League Club, the Taxpayers' Union, and the Citizens'
Association. The urban bourgeoisie advocated property rights and

free and untrammeled markets. With growing confidence and anxiety, they pursued suffrage restrictions along class lines. They dominated culture as well, building such new cultural institutions as the New York Philharmonic Orchestra and the Metropolitan Museum of Art.

The postwar era was also the golden age of New York society. Bourgeois New York embraced a conspicuous display of wealth, following the lead provided by Parisians. Empress Eugenie of France became the model for fashion. Some wealthy women ordered forty dresses at a time from Paris, each worth as much as $2,500. Yet the urban bourgeoisie could also shop well at home. Rowland Macy expanded his department store. By 1870, one could also shop at Lord and Taylor, F. A. O. Schwarz, and Tiffany's. And there was money to spend. William Astor and Alexander T. Stuart had incomes over a million dollars. At one celebrated meal at Delmonico's, the female guests found gold bracelets hidden in their napkins.

Prosperity, however, failed to overcome poverty. New factories attracted workers and heightened the demand for available housing. Living conditions in the manufacturing sections of New York deteriorated. On the Lower East Side, Irish and German workers suffered poor public sanitation. In the worst areas, the death rate in 1866 reached 195 per thousand. Clinging tenaciously to his free-labor values, Greeley saw no excuse for poverty: the pauper should and could work himself out of his condition. In Greeley's view, such a person was not taking advantage of the opportunities provided by a free America.

Class stratification and increasing class and ethnic conflict followed. On July 12, 1871, Protestant Irishmen brazenly walked through the Catholic neighborhoods on Eighth Avenue. The ensuing Orange Riot left sixty-two New Yorkers dead. The New York bourgeoisie watched these developments warily, fearing that their city would reenact the Paris Commune of that year.

Industrialization and the growth of a wage-earning working class triggered a resurgence of the labor movement in New York. According to urban historians Edwin G. Burrows and Mike Wallace, "A larger proportion of the metropolitan working population enrolled in trade unions between 1865 and 1873 than during any other period of the nineteenth century." In 1861, there were about fifteen unions in New York City; by 1864, there were 157.

The transformation of work from independent producers to wage earners intensified rapidly. The harmony of employer and employee so dear to Greeley was now being replaced by bitter conflict. "It is one of the misfortunes of the times," noted the *United States Economist and Dry Goods Reporter* in 1868, "that . . . antagonism has arisen between capital and labor in place of the feeling of identity of interests which should exist." German immigrant socialists believed only an attack on the capitalist system itself would solve labor's problem. In New York, the Marxist International Workingmen's Association claimed five thousand members by 1871.

Horace Greeley had long enjoyed a reputation as a friend of labor. He was often the key speaker at workers' meetings. The New York chapter of the Knights of St. Crispin made the *Tribune* its state organ. Yet Greeley was alienated by the tenor of labor activism after the Civil War. One historian has estimated that there were 249 strikes in New York between 1863 and 1873. Greeley was especially hostile to strikes, maintaining that capital had the right to hire and fire as it saw fit. He spelled out his reasons in a *Tribune* editorial from 1867 titled "Conspiracy in Labor." He began with the assumption that "personal independence is the quality that gives dignity and insures success to American industry." Strikes were a foolish way "as a means of adjusting Labor and Capital." They were a waste of valuable industrial time and took the savings of workers that could be used for social betterment. During a strike, Greeley argued, the worker "learns nothing. He enriches no faculty. He gains no influence." Perhaps worst of all, strikes threatened the concordant relationship between workers and employers so valued by Greeley: "An intense and bitter selfishness takes the place of the sentimental kindnesses of the ancient dispensation and from either party nobleness disappears." Postwar labor conflict, rooted in starker class divisions and exhibiting greater class consciousness, undermined Greeley's Whiggish vision of an orderly and harmonious economic order. Yet he continued to pay homage to an economic and social vision of the early republic.

In May 1865, the Workingmen's Union in New York launched a campaign to reduce the working day to eight hours. The eight-hour day became the masthead for labor reform during Reconstruction. The New York state legislature in April 1867 passed an eight-hour bill that was supported by both reformist Radical Republicans and Democrats. Greeley opposed the eight-hour movement, deeming it "clearly desirable though not yet practicable, as we trust it may be in 'the good time coming.'" Adverse to any class view of the labor situation, Greeley persisted in his belief in free labor mobility: "We hold that a portion presently and nine-tenths ultimately of the Laboring Class may become their own masters if they will." An eight-hour day would become irrelevant when workers become their own employers and could regulate their own hours.

Just as he had during the 1840s, Greeley placed his faith for labor in cooperative movements. "In our judgment," Greeley wrote, "COOPERATION is the true watchword and sheet-anchor of Labor." Greeley believed that labor in any of the craft trades should form "combinations," in which workers would pool together their savings to procure the means of production. Greeley insisted that cooperation was "a widespread and steady revolution in the industrial world." Paris already had thirty such industrial associations.

Greeley described how cooperation would work: "If one hundred carpenters will organize a cooperative body, elect proper and upright officers, adopt suitable rules and regulations, and pay into the general fund from $15 to $25 each, beside the use of each man's chest of tools, they may therewith procure and equip a shop, and become their own employers, increase their general usefulness to their families and to society, improve their character as workmen and their position in the social scale, and secure at all times reasonable prices for the results of their labor." The value of cooperation, he added, would go beyond economic benefits. Always tending to conflate economic with social progress, Greeley insisted that it would lead to the regeneration of the working class. "Testimony goes to show," he explained, "that the members become more frugal, persevering, grave, temperate, and domestic. Their influence on the general class of working people is excellent. They form a species of labor aristocracy into which it becomes a privilege to enter."

IV

The post–Civil War transformation of New York was political as well as economic. Perhaps the most notable development was the rise of the "Tweed Ring," a powerful but corrupt urban political machine. William Marcy Tweed was a former chairmaker who had become the boss of Tammany Hall, the Democratic organization. Tweed's company included such figures as Peter B. Sweeny, "Slippery Dick" Connolly, and "Elegant Oakey" Hall. In the 1866 election, Tammany supported John T. Hoffman for governor. The machine was joined by Greeley's archnemesis Thurlow Weed. To oppose Hoffman, New York Republicans ran Reuben E. Fenton. Greeley was a candidate for Congress from New York City, but lost by a majority vote of almost ten thousand. In 1870, Tweed proposed a new charter for the city that would have given control of the city to his cabal. Greeley opposed what he saw as an overreach of political power.

By the spring of 1871, the Tweed Ring began to unravel when accusations of fraud regarding the bonded debt became public. On September 3, 1871, elite New Yorkers assembled and established the Committee of Citizens and Taxpayers for the Financial Reform of the City and the County of New York. They formed an operating Committee of Seventy that attacked Tweed Ring, becoming the vanguard of bourgeois urban reform. Their goal was to restructure city government to give men of property more power. They proposed to limit suffrage and advocated a scheme of "minority representation" to counter the political mobilization of workers.

On the state level, the split between Weed and Greeley continued to shape New York politics. On November 14, 1866, Greeley announced himself as a candidate for the Senate in the next year's election. He ran against Charles Folger, Reuben E. Fenton, Roscoe Conkling, Noah Davis, and Lyman Tremaine. Conkling was supported by Weed. Greeley counted on the support of Radical Republicans, but lost their backing by declaring for universal amnesty. The nomination went to Conkling. Yet Greeley remained a leader in the Republican Party and was chosen to read the resolutions at a Republican rally at Cooper Union on October 16, 1867.

He still hungered for office. In 1868, he presented himself as candidate for governor. He was supported by Fenton's followers, but Conkling stopped the movement. Nonetheless, Greeley worked hard in the 1868 campaign against the Democrat Hoffman, attacking Tammany Hall for fraudulent voter registrations. In the fall elections, the Republican Ulysses S. Grant won the presidency, although New York City Republicans were defeated. In 1870, Greeley ran once more for Congress in the Sixth Congressional District, but lost to Samuel Sullivan "Sunset" Cox.

Greeley was an active participant at the New York Constitutional Convention of 1867, which convened at Albany on June 4. For years, Radical Republicans in New York had been calling for a constitutional convention. One historian has called Greeley "probably the most outspoken advocate of constitutional reform in the state." Greeley won election to the convention as an at-large delegate from Westchester County. Once again, he was an advocate for reform and economy in government who needlessly alienated his fellow delegates with ill-considered and ill-timed ideas. As one of his biographers describes it, "The good ship *Reform* seemed fated to run into head winds when it set sail for the Promised Land with pilot Greeley at its helm." For instance, Greeley attacked fellow Republicans for canal frauds and expressed his annoyance with their poor attendance and often lack of quorums at the convention. He opposed Friday-to-Tuesday adjournments. Not surprisingly, all his reform proposals went down to defeat.

Greeley's major role at the New York Constitutional Convention was as chair of the Committee on the Right of Suffrage and the Qualifications to Hold Office. In Albany, he continued his commitment to black suffrage. In the end, Democratic opponents of equal voting rights were able to put the issue on a separate ballot where it failed. In his role as committee chair, Greeley also confronted the question of women's suffrage. In 1848, Greeley had thought female suffrage unwise but acknowledged it was "the assertion of a natural right and as such must be conceded." He had also supported the right of women to speak in public at the World Temperance Convention that met in New York in 1853.

Elizabeth Cady Stanton considered Greeley "one of our most faithful champions." At a universal suffrage convention in New York, she placed Greeley among a group that stood "on the high mountain-top of humanity." Yet their relationship later soured. In 1864, she insisted that she be referred to as "Elizabeth Cady Stanton," but he insisted on calling her "Mrs. Henry Stanton." The *Tribune* refused to support the Equal Suffrage Convention meeting in New York, although it did endorse a referendum on women's suffrage being considered in Kansas.

At the New York Constitutional Convention, Greeley encountered Susan B. Anthony and Stanton. His committee turned down their plea, despite the efforts of Molly Greeley, who had submitted a petition signed by twenty-eight thousand men and women. Greeley and the *Tribune* expressed their views against women's suffrage. They claimed that to "make women voters at our elections as now held, and eligible to office in competition with men, would be far better calculated to corrupt Woman than to reform and purify our politics."

V

"That Horace Greeley should be nominated by a Democratic convention," wrote a surprised Trenton (New Jersey) *True American* in 1872, "seems nothing less than a political miracle, which nothing but a most extraordinary condition of public affairs and an equally extraordinary condition of public feeling consequent thereon could have been brought about." Running for the presidency in 1872 as a Liberal Republican (and later endorsed by the Democrats) was the last public crusade for Horace Greeley. In many ways, Greeley's alliance with the Liberal Republicans marked his retreat from Reconstruction. After years of fighting for black suffrage and civil rights (enshrined in the Fourteenth and Fifteenth Amendments), he accepted a more laissez-faire approach to the postwar South by advocating universal amnesty for former Confederates.

The Liberal Republican movement was born in Missouri. Republican Carl Schurz, a former German Forty-Eighter and active abolitionist who served as a wartime general and minister to Spain, was one of its founders. The other was B. Gratz Brown, a former Whig and editor of the Missouri *Democrat* who was elected senator in 1863. In 1870, Schurz and Brown won in Missouri on a platform of universal amnesty, tariff reform, and opposition to the Grant administration. This splinter movement within the Republican Party was led by a group of editors known as the "Quatrilateral": Samuel Bowles of the Springfield *Republican*, Horace White of the *Chicago Daily Tribune*, Murat Halstead of the Cincinnati *Commercial*, and Henry Watterson of the Louisville *Courier-Journal*.

The coalition that gathered around the Liberal Republicans was an odd assortment of New England patricians, free traders, civil service reformers, former free soilers, and agrarian radicals. Liberals also supported the New Departure in the South, a surface acceptance of the Civil War amendments accompanied by a return to white conservative rule. The Liberal Republican movement was strengthened by currents of liberal thought that gained ascendancy in New York during the late 1860s. In 1865, Simon Sterne and Alexander Delmar founded the *New York Social Science Review* based on the intellectual foundations of Herbert Spencer and free-trade economics. Liberal thinking reflected the rise of the urban middle class. In their journal, Sterne and Delmar considered electoral measures to ensure the dominance of a small minority elite in a political order of universal suffrage. Delmar would work for Greeley in 1872.

The increasingly scandal-ridden administration of President Grant strengthened the Liberal Republican movement. The Democratic *Cincinnati Enquirer* warned of the "alarming corruption which has involved every branch of the Civil Service, the example of which has been set by Grant himself, by his shameful nepotism and acceptance of bribes." The *Hartford Times* spoke of "the most lawless, centralizing, and corrupt Administration which this country has ever known." Corruption seeped into government councils by the lax oversight of patronage. Grant made the mistake of being seen with Jay Gould and Jim Fisk while the pair were attempting to corner the gold market in 1868.

Greeley was alienated from Grant, largely due to the president's handling of patronage in New York. Grant sided with Conkling over

Fenton. For Greeley, the issue of patronage peaked when Grant appointed Conklingite Thomas Murphy for collector of the Port of New York. By the summer of 1871, Greeley was openly opposing Grant's renomination and becoming more vocal about civil service reform. The next year, for example, the *Tribune* wrote of the "depraved and cynical disregard for even the appearance of public conscience which has become of late so dangerous a characteristic of the Administration." On March 7, 1872, Greeley wrote to the chairman of the Republican National Committee, essentially withdrawing himself from the party. Greeley's only obstacle to joining the Liberals—and it was not a small one—was their stance on free trade.

On May 1, the Liberal Republican convention opened in Cincinnati. According to the *New York Tribune*, there had "never been a better class of men gathered on such an occasion, and rarely as much willingness to forego [sic] personal preference for the sake of making a strong ticket." The Convention Address blamed President Grant for allowing corruption to poison his administration and accused the Republican Party of not pursuing justice in this regard. "The Administration now in power," the Liberals declared, "has rendered itself guilty of wanton disregard of the laws of the land, and of usurping powers not granted by the Constitution." It has degraded itself and the Republican Party, "once justly entitled to the confidence of the nation, by a base sycophancy to the dispenser of the Executive power and patronage, unworthy of republican freemen."

The resolutions passed by the Cincinnati convention included equality before the law; the settlement of the Civil War issues by the Thirteenth, Fourteenth, and Fifteenth Amendments; the removal of all disabilities on Southern whites; the granting of suffrage decisions to the states; and the condemnation of civil service as "a mere instrument of partisan tyranny and personal ambition, and an object of selfish greed." The Liberal Republican platform also endorsed public credit and a return to specie payment, while opposing further grants to railroads and corporations. "No broader or simpler creed was ever promulgated," claimed the *Tribune*: "Liberty, honesty, and peace, against centralization, corruption, and perpetual war." Sympathetic Democratic papers agreed. The

Hartford Times spoke about casting aside "the dead issues of the past." Sectional reconciliation was close at hand, the *Cincinnati Enquirer* hoped, "and once more we shall be a united confederacy and a free people."

Along with creating a platform, the main order of business at the Cincinnati convention was the nomination of a presidential candidate to run against Grant in the fall. By January 1872, Greeley's name was being mentioned as a possible choice. B. Gratz Brown was the leading candidate, but was hampered by a reputation as an alcoholic. The major candidates besides Brown were Charles Francis Adams of Massachusetts, Lyman Trumbull and David Davis of Illinois, and Andrew G. Curtin of Pennsylvania. By April, Greeley had the backing of sixty-four of sixty-eight New York delegates. Whitelaw Reid, who was already working for the *Tribune*, went to Cincinnati to lay the groundwork for Greeley's nomination.

On the first few ballots, Greeley ran second to Adams. On the sixth ballot, Greeley went ahead. The *Tribune* editor responded to his nomination on May 20, 1872, with the affirmation that "the movement which found expression at Cincinnati has received the stamp of public approval, and been hailed by a majority of our countrymen as the harbinger of a better day for the Republic."

Greeley's nomination received a mixed reaction throughout the nation. There was clearly enthusiasm in some corners. Both St. Louis and New Orleans witnessed a run on white hats (characteristically worn by Greeley) as a response to his nomination. Greeley was endorsed by the radical African American New Orleans *Tribune*: "No man has done more to liberate the colored people of this country and ameliorate their condition than Mr. Greeley. And his labors have been just as earnestly given for the benefit and advancement of the white laboring classes." From the white South, the editor of the Columbia (South Carolina) *Phoenix* assured Greeley that he had "a lot of warm admirers among the Democrats of the South, for we feel that you have befriended us in the day of our humiliation and suffering, when friends were few."

Yet the negative response from the press to Greeley's nomination was equal, if not stronger. "Probably there never before was an occasion," claimed the Baltimore *American*, "when the mere fact of a man's candidacy elicited so many insuperable objections to him." James Parton, Greeley's first biographer, recalled that the editor's nomination "was received with an explosion of caricature and burlesque, which continued through the canvass." The *Evening Wisconsin* believed "there is such a pervading distrust of his executive ability and sagacity, that, while all rather like him, very few will vote for him for President." The Milwaukee *Sentinel* worried about Greeley's lack of executive ability and his willful personality. The Knoxville *Chronicle* raised another point about "his peculiar traits of character," arguing that his "eccentricities are weak points in his character and make him exceedingly vulnerable as a candidate."

The Liberal Republican candidate occasioned surprise along with criticism. In particular, how would the party reconcile its advocacy of free trade with a candidate who supported a tariff? "The thing is supremely ridiculous," pointed out the Chicago *Journal*, "Horace Greeley, the Protectionist *par excellence*, striking hands with Gratz Brown, the notorious *Free Trader*, and becoming the candidate of a Convention of Free Traders!" On this contentious question, Greeley himself recommended that it be "treated as the people's immediate business, to be shaped and directed by them through their representatives in Congress." The solution arrived at by the Liberal Republicans was simply to allow both positions within the new party. "We have steadfastly insisted," wrote the *Tribune*, "that the liberty to differ on this question always hitherto enjoyed and exercised by Republicans shall not be denied to those who sympathize with the Liberal movements."

Lacking a viable candidate with national appeal, the Democratic Party endorsed Greeley at its national convention in Baltimore in June. This gave him the distinction of being the first person nominated for the presidency by two different parties. The New Jersey *American Standard* gave its "unqualified adherence" to Greeley and his running mate Brown. "He has strengthened the weak," argued another Democratic journal, "he has lifted the fallen, he has defended religious liberty, he has seen a white soul under a dark skin, he has been steadfast to his faith to freedom during all the 40 years of his active life." Yet for many Democrats, Greeley was hard to swallow. As a Whig and then a Republican, the *Tribune* editor had been attacking Democrats for decades. Additionally, his embrace of a wide variety of reforms, his antislavery, and his protectionism had alienated many Democrats.

"We shall count on 120 electoral votes from the South, and hope for 64 more from the north," Greeley wrote confidently on June 24, 1872. Perhaps more realistically, he promised to "do our best." The Liberal/Democratic campaign began with enthusiasm. Harking back to the election of 1840, voters could sing and dance to the "Greeley Galop," the "Greeley Marseillaise," and selections from the *Farmer of Chappaqua Songster*. In New York City, there was an Eighteenth Assembly District Greeley Republican Association on the East Side and a Greeley and Brown German Nineteenth Ward Club. Greeley pressed forward with civil service reform. "The abuses of patronage multiply," he claimed; "the new rules and regulations are suspended before they have fairly been tried." The *Tribune* also lauded the New Departure movement in the South as a way to put sectionalism to rest: "Henceforth North and South are united as one country, animated by the same patriotism and pursuing the same aims."

By the 1872 campaign, Greeley had seemed to join the retreat from Reconstruction that was becoming evident in the North. In May, he spoke to the black community in Poughkeepsie, New York, as a benefit for the African Methodist Episcopal Zion church there. Acknowledging that blacks were to be a part of the American body politic, Greeley nonetheless criticized New York's blacks and urged self-help instead of reliance upon government intervention. He believed they were "inclined to lean on and expect help from other races, beyond what is reasonable and beyond what is wholesome." Greeley himself even bragged about the harsh ways he treated beggars on the streets of New York. The former Associationist and land reformer was now sounding like a champion of the New York bourgeoisie.

As summer progressed, the attacks on Greeley increased. He was denounced as "Old Chappaquack" and lampooned in the cartoons of Thomas Nast, a popular political cartoonist in post–Civil War America sympathetic to the views of the Radical Republicans. Mark Twain recalled that Nast's drawings played a major role in his defeat. Grant claimed similarly that one of the factors in his victory was "the pencil of Thomas Nast."

Greeley was attacked from the other side of the political spectrum by former abolitionists. Lydia Maria Child considered him a "tool in the hands of Southern despots, and their unprincipled allies, the Democrats." William Lloyd Garrison insisted that Greeley was "a man without any fixed principles." Northern intellectuals like historian George Bancroft thought Greeley would attract the "worst elements in our society." Legal scholar Francis Leiber saw in Greeley's nomination a "presumptuous mediocrity and inanity."

Other problems afflicted the Greeley campaign. In May 1872, Congress passed an amnesty bill that undercut one of the central planks in the Liberal platform. As the potent and wealthy Republican political machine mobilized into action, the party won early victories in Maine and Vermont. Still, Greeley made more than two hundred speeches on a campaign tour.

In the end, Greeley won Georgia, Kentucky, Maryland, Missouri, Tennessee, and Texas. Yet he was soundly defeated by President Grant, who carried every state in the North. In the final count, Grant won by a popular majority of over 760,000. This 56 percent margin was the highest of any presidential candidate between 1828 and 1904.

VI

The election of 1872 left Greeley defeated and embittered. That summer, Greeley's wife Molly returned ill from a European trip. Most of her teeth were already gone. Suffering from consumption, she stayed at the home of friend and publisher Alvin J. Johnson. Horace was with her almost every night. Molly Greeley died on October 30. "I am not dead but wish I were," Horace wrote to a friend. "My house is desolate, my future dark." The very next day, he learned of his humiliating defeat by Grant.

On top of his wife's death and his political ill fortune, Greeley was in financial trouble. He was forced to write Commodore Vanderbilt for financial help, since Vanderbilt's son had once borrowed money from Greeley for gambling.

It was all proving too much for Greeley. His mental health deteriorated quickly. James Parton recalled that he "uttered wild words about business and about the election." Some of Greeley's friends urged that he be institutionalized in a hospital for the mentally insane. "I stand naked before my God," Greeley said in one of his last statements, "the most utterly, hopelessly wretched and undone of all who ever lived."

He was moved to a sanitarium in Pleasantville, New York, where he died at 6:50 p.m. on Friday, November 29, 1872. His daughters and his fellow editor Whitelaw Reid were at his side. Greeley's body lay at the home of his friend Samuel Sinclair until December 3, when it was moved to the Governor's Room in City Hall. Services were held at the Universalist Church of the Divine Paternity on December 4. Henry Ward Beecher, brother of the author of *Uncle Tom's Cabin*, delivered the eulogy. Greeley was buried in Green-Wood Cemetery in Brooklyn.

VII

It would not be long before Horace Greeley began to receive his due as a significant figure in American history. In 1888, the Horace Greeley Post 577 of the Grand Army of the Republic campaigned for a statue of the *Tribune* editor. The statue was finally unveiled on May 30, 1894. It sits today at the busy corner of Broadway/Sixth Avenue and 32nd Street in New York. Other monuments testify to the variety of Greeley's interests and accomplishments. In 1942, the liberty ship *Horace Greeley* was launched. In 1947, Vermont, the birthplace of Horace Greeley, dedicated the Horace Greeley Memorial Highway. In 1961, the U.S. Postal Service issued a stamp of Greeley in its "Famous American Series." Today, there is a city named Greeley in Colorado, Kansas, Missouri, Nebraska, and even South Carolina. Sturdy hikers can walk out to Greeley Point in Wyoming.

As a reformer, politician, and editor, Greeley boldly grappled with the two central pressing problems of his age: slavery and the rise of industrial capitalism. Perhaps as much as any other person, Horace Greeley embodied the dynamism and ambiguities of the United States during the mid-nineteenth century. He displayed both the potentials and problems of a democratic society moving into modernity.

Bibliography

Primary Sources

Manuscripts

Library of Congress, Washington, D.C.

- Horace Greeley Papers
- Whitelaw Reid Papers
- Carl Schurz Papers

New York Historical Society, New York, New York

- Horace Greeley Papers

New York Public Library, New York, New York

- Greeley-Colfax Correspondence
- Horace Greeley Papers

University of Rochester, Rush Rhees Library, Rochester, New York

- Greeley-Seward Correspondence
- Horace Greeley Papers
- Thurlow Weed Papers

Newspapers

Jeffersonian
Log Cabin
New-Yorker
New York Tribune

Published Primary Sources

Greeley, Horace. *An Overland Journey from New York to San Francisco in the Summer of 1859.* Edited, and with notes and an introduction, by Charles T. Duncan. New York: Alfred A. Knopf, 1964.

———. *Recollections of a Busy Life.* New York: J. B. Ford & Co., 1868.

Marx, Karl. *Dispatches for the* New York Tribune: *Selected Journalism of Karl Marx.* Edited by James Ledbetter, with a foreword by Francis Wheen. New York: Penguin, 2007.

SECONDARY SOURCES

Albion, Robert Greenhalgh. *The Rise of New York Port* [1815–1860]. New York: Charles Scribner's Sons, 1939.

Anbinder, Tyler G. *Nativism and Slavery: The Northern Know Nothings and the Politics of the 1850s.* New York: Oxford University Press, 1992.

Ashworth, John. *"Agrarians" and "Aristocrats": Party Political Ideology in the United States, 1837–1846.* Cambridge: Cambridge University Press, 1983.

Baldasty, Gerald J. *The Commercialization of News in the Nineteenth Century.* Madison: University of Wisconsin Press, 1992.

Baum, Dale, and Dale T. Knobel. "Anatomy of a Realignment: New York Presidential Politics, 1848–1860." *New York History* 65 (1984): 61–81.

Beckert, Sven. *The Monied Metropolis: New York City and the Consolidation of the American Bourgeoisie, 1850–1896.* New York: Cambridge University Press, 2001.

Bernstein, Iver. *The New York City Draft Riots: Their Significance for American Society and Politics in the Age of the Civil War.* New York: Oxford University Press, 1990.

Bestor, Arthur. "Albert Brisbane: Propagandist for Socialism in the 1840s." *New York History* 28 (1947): 128–58.

Billington, Ray Allen. *The Protestant Crusade, 1800–1860: A Study of the Origins of American Nativism*. New York: Rinehart, 1938.

Bronstein, Jamie L. *Land Reform and Working-Class Experience in Britain and the United States, 1800–1862*. Stanford, Calif.: Stanford University Press, 1999.

Burrows, Edwin G., and Mike Wallace. *Gotham: A History of New York City to 1898*. New York: Oxford University Press, 1999.

Butler, Leslie. *Critical Americans: Victorian Intellectuals and Transatlantic Liberal Reform*. Chapel Hill: University of North Carolina Press, 2007.

Callow, Alexander B., Jr. *The Tweed Ring*. New York: Oxford University Press, 1966.

Capper, Charles. *Margaret Fuller: An American Romantic Life*. Two vols. New York: Oxford University Press, 1992–2008.

Carman, Henry J., and Reinhard H. Luthin. "The Seward-Fillmore Feud and the Disruption of the Whig Party." *New York History* 24 (1943): 335–57.

Clark, Christopher. *Social Change in America from the Revolution through the Civil War*. Chicago: Ivan R. Dee, 2006.

Conley, Patrick T. *Democracy in Decline: Rhode Island's Constitutional Development, 1776–1841*. Providence: Rhode Island Historical Society, 1977.

Crouthamel, James L. *Bennett's New York Herald and the Rise of the Popular Press*. Syracuse, N.Y.: Syracuse University Press, 1989.

Dannenbaum, Jed. *Drink and Disorder: Temperance Reform in Cincinnati from the Washington Revival to the WCTU*. Urbana: University of Illinois Press, 1984.

Donald, David H. *Charles Sumner and the Rights of Man*. Boston: Little, Brown, 1970.

Donald, David H., Jean Harvey Baker, and Michael F. Holt. *The Civil War and Reconstruction*. New York: Norton, 2001.

Downey, Mathew T. "Horace Greeley and the Politicians: The Liberal Republican Convention in 1872." *Journal of American History* 53 (1967): 727–50.

Ellis, David Maldwyn. *Landlords and Tenants in the Hudson-Mohawk Region, 1790–1850*. Ithaca, N.Y.: Cornell University Press, 1946.

Eyal, Yonatan. "Charles Eliot Norton, E. L. Godkin, and the Liberal Republicans of 1872." *American Nineteenth Century History* 2 (Spring 2001): 53–74.

———. *The Young America Movement and the Transformation of the Democratic Party, 1828–1861*. Cambridge: Cambridge University Press, 2007.

Fahrney, Ralph Ray. *Horace Greeley and the* Tribune *in the Civil War.* Cedar Rapids, Iowa: Torch Press, 1936. Reprint, New York: De Capo, 1970.

Foner, Eric. *Free Soil, Free Labor, Free Men: The Ideology of the Republican Party before the Civil War.* New York: Oxford University Press, 1970.

Foner, Philip S. *Business and Slavery: The New York Merchants and the Irrepressible Conflict.* Chapel Hill: University of North Carolina Press, 1941.

Formisano, Ronald P. *For the People: American Populist Movements from the Revolution to the 1850s.* Chapel Hill: University of North Carolina Press, 2008.

Garraty, John. *Silas Wright.* New York: Columbia University Press, 1949.

Gettleman, Marvin E. *The Dorr Rebellion: A Study in American Radicalism, 1833–1849.* New York: Random House, 1973.

Gienapp, William E. *The Origins of the Republican Party, 1852–1856.* New York: Oxford University Press, 1987.

Guarneri, Carl J. *Utopian Alternative: Fourierism in Nineteenth-Century America.* Ithaca, N.Y.: Cornell University Press, 1999.

Gunderson, Robert B. *The Log-Cabin Campaign.* Lexington: University of Kentucky Press, 1957.

Harper, Robert. *Lincoln and the Press.* New York: McGraw-Hill, 1951.

Hesseltine, William B. *Lincoln and the War Governors.* New York: Alfred A. Knopf, 1948.

Holt, Michael Fitzgibbon. *Forging a Majority: The Formation of the Republican Party in Pittsburgh, 1848–1860.* New Haven, Conn.: Yale University Press, 1969.

———. *The Rise and Fall of the American Whig Party: Jacksonian Politics and the Onset of the Civil War.* New York: Oxford University Press, 1999.

Horner, Harlan. *Lincoln and Greeley.* Urbana: University of Illinois Press, 1953.

Howe, Daniel Walker. *The Political Culture of the American Whigs.* Chicago: University of Chicago Press, 1979.

———. *The Unitarian Conscience: Harvard Moral Philosophy, 1805–1861.* Cambridge, Mass.: Harvard University Press, 1970.

———. *What Hath God Wrought: The Transformation of America, 1815–1848.* New York: Oxford University Press, 2007.

Huston, Reeve. *Land and Freedom: Rural Society, Popular Protest, and Party Politics in Antebellum New York.* New York: Oxford University Press, 2000.

Isely, Jeter A. *Horace Greeley and the Republican Party, 1853–1861: A Study of the* New York Tribune. Princeton, N.J.: Princeton University Press, 1947.

Kohl, Lawrence Frederick. *The Politics of Individualism: Parties and the American Character in the Jacksonian Era.* New York: Oxford University Press, 1989.

McPherson, James. "Grant or Greeley? The Abolitionist Dilemma in the Election of 1872." *American Historical Review* 71 (1965): 43–61.

Messer-Kruse, Timothy. *Yankee International: Marxism and the American Reform Tradition, 1848–1876.* Chapel Hill: University of North Carolina Press, 1998.

Mohr, James. *The Radical Republicans and Reform in New York during Reconstruction.* Ithaca, N.Y.: Cornell University Press, 1973.

Mott, Frank Luther. *American Journalism: A History of American Newspapers in the United States through 260 Years, 1690–1950.* Rev. ed. New York: Macmillan, 1950.

Neeley, Mark E. *The Union Divided: Party Conflict in the Civil War North.* Cambridge, Mass.: Harvard University Press, 2002.

Nevins, Allan. *The Emergence of Lincoln.* Two vols. New York: Scribner, 1950.

———. *Ordeal of the Union.* Two vols. New York: Scribner, 1947.

———. *The War for the Union.* Four vols. New York: Scribner, 1959–1971.

Potter, David. "Horace Greeley and Peaceable Secession." *Journal of Southern History* 7 (1941): 145–59.

———. *Lincoln and His Party in the Secession Crisis.* New Haven, Conn.: Yale University Press, 1942.

Quigly, David. *Second Founding: New York City, Reconstruction, and the Making of American Democracy.* New York: Hill & Wang, 2004.

Ross, Earle Dudley. *The Liberal Republican Movement.* New York: H. Holt & Co., 1919.

Saxton, Alexander. "Problems of Class and Race in the Origins of the Mass Circulation Press." *American Quarterly* 36 (1984): 211–34.

Schiller, Dan. *Objectivity and the News: The Public and the Rise of Commercial Journalism.* Philadelphia: University of Pennsylvania Press, 1981.

Schudson, Michael. *Discovering the News: A Social History of American Newspapers.* New York: Basic Books, 1978.

Sharp, James Roger. *The Jacksonians versus the Banks: Politics in the States after the Panic of 1837.* New York: Columbia University Press, 1970.

Stampp, Kenneth M. *And the War Came: The North and the Secession Crisis, 1860–1861.* Baton Rouge: Louisiana State University Press, 1950.

Stebbins, Homer A. *A Political History of the State of New York State, 1865–1869*. New York: Columbia University Press, 1913.

Steele, Janet. *The Sun Shines for All: Journalism and Ideology in the Life of Charles A. Dana*. Syracuse, N.Y.: Syracuse University Press, 1993.

Trefousse, Hans L. *The Radical Republicans: Lincoln's Vanguard for Social Justice*. New York: Alfred A. Knopf, 1969.

Tuchinsky, Adam-Max. *Horace Greeley's* New-York Tribune: *Civil War–Era Socialism and the Crisis of Free Labor*. Ithaca, N.Y.: Cornell University Press, 2009.

Tyler, Alice Felt. *Freedom's Ferment: Phases of American Social History to 1860*. Minneapolis: University of Minnesota Press, 1944.

Van Deusen, Glyndon. *Horace Greeley, Nineteenth-Century Crusader*. Philadelphia: University of Pennsylvania Press, 1953.

———. *Thurlow Weed: Wizard of the Lobby*. Boston: Little, Brown, 1947.

———. *William Henry Seward*. New York: Oxford University Press, 1967.

Widmer, Edward L. *Young America: The Flowering of Democracy in New York City*. New York: Oxford University Press, 1999.

Wilentz, Sean. *Chants Democratic: New York City and the Rise of the American Working Class, 1788–1850*. New York: Oxford University Press, 1984.

———. *The Rise of American Democracy: Jefferson to Lincoln*. New York: Norton, 2005.

Williams, Robert C. *Horace Greeley: Champion of American Freedom*. New York: New York University Press, 2006.

Wittke, Carl. *Refugees of Revolution: The German Forty-Eighters in America*. Philadelphia: University of Pennsylvania Press, 1952.

Wood, Gordon S. *Empire of Liberty: A History of the Early Republic, 1789–1815*. New York: Oxford University Press, 2009.

Zahler, Helene Sara. *Eastern Workingmen and National Land Policy, 1829–1862*. New York: Columbia University Press, 1941.

Index

abolitionism, 38–39, 40–41, 66, 90, 99, 106, 118, 141, 147, 152, 158. *See also* slavery controversy

Adams, Charles Francis, 106, 152, 177

Adams, John Quincy, 12, 23, 34, 106

Address on the Right of Free Suffrage (1832), 81. *See also* Luther, Seth

Alaska, purchase of, 166

Albany *Evening Journal*, 43, 117

Albany *Freeholder*, 77

"Albany Regency," 23

Amana, 65

American Monthly Magazine, 35, 61

American Union of Associationists, 70. *See also* Fourierism

Amherst (New Hampshire), 1, 9, 13

Anthony, Susan B., 99, 174

Antietam, Battle of, 142

Appeal to the Colored Citizens of the World (1829), 38. *See also* Walker, David

anti-Masonry, 13–14, 26, 28

Anti-Rent War (New York), 66, 75–79, 85

Anti-Renter, 77

Associated Press, 51

Associationism, 67–72, 75, 171. *See also* Fourierism

Astor, William, 169

BUS (Second Bank of the United States), 25–26, 32, 44

Ballou, Hosea, 15, 72

Bancroft, George, 180

Banks, Nathaniel, 116, 123

"Barnburners," 89, 90, 100, 105

Barnum, P. T., 5, 8

Bates, Edward, 128, 129

Beach, Alfred Ely, 168

Bear, John W., 21

Bebb, William, 105

Bedford, New Hampshire, 13

Beecher, Henry Ward, 49, 181

Bell, John C., 129

Bennett, James Gordon, 53, 167

Benton, Thomas Hart, 34, 123

Bernstein, Iver, 144
Biddle, Nicholas, 25, 44
Birney, James G., 87
Black Codes, 163. *See also*
    Reconstruction
Blackwell, Antoinette Brown, 99
Blaine, James G., 107
Blair, Francis P., 25
Bliss, Amos, 10
Booth, John Wilkes, 153
Botts, John Minor, 104, 160
Bovary, Alvan, 116
Bowles, Samuel, 125, 175
Bragg, Braxton, 41
Bragg, William, 41
Breckinridge, John C., 129
Brisbane, Albert, 50, 69, 75. *See
    also Social Destiny of Man*
Brook Farm, 57, 65
Brooks, Henry Sands, 18
Brooks, James, 143
Brooks Brothers, 18, 144
Brown, B. Gratz, 175, 177, 178
Brown, John, 127
Brownson, Orestes, 36, 82
Bryant, William Cullen, 18, 59,
    82, 136, 150
Buchanan, James, 123, 124, 125
Bull Run (Manassas), Battle of,
    138, 139
Burrows, Edwin G., 169–70
Butler, Benjamin, 150

Calhoun, John C., 23, 25, 86, 100,
    110
California: Greeley's trip to, 126–
    27; statehood, 109–10, 123
Cambreleng, Churchill C., 82
Canandaigua, New York, 13
Carey, Henry C., 31
Carlyle, Thomas, 73. *See also Past
    and Present*

Cass, Lewis, 106, 114
Chandler, Zachariah, 139
Channing, William Henry, 70, 75
Chappaqua (New York), 57, 137,
    155, 157
Chase, Salmon P., 134, 162
Chicago *Daily Tribune*, 175
Child, Lydia Maria, 115, 180
Cincinnati *Commercial*, 175
Citizen's Association (New York),
    168
civil service reform, 157, 175–76,
    179
Clapp, Henry, 5
Clark, John C., 43
Clarke, James Freeman, 58
classical literature, in *Tribune*, 62
Clay, Henry, 23, 25, 27–28, 33,
    38, 44, 100–102, 104–5, 110
Clay Tribune, 86
Clymer (Pennsylvania), 11
Coggeshall, James, 54
Cole, A. N., 116
Cole, Thomas, 18
Colfax, Schuyler, 116, 124, 166
Columbia (South Carolina)
    Phoenix, 177
Columbian Orator, 9
Commercial Advertiser (New York),
    16
Committee of Citizens and
    Taxpayers for the Financial
    Reform of the City and the
    County of New York, 172
Committee of Thirty-Three, 134
Compromise of 1850, 110–11
Confederate States of America,
    establishment of, 132–33. *See
    also* secession crisis
confiscation, 164. *See also*
    Reconstruction
Conkling, Roscoe, 172

Connolly, "Slippery Dick," 172
Conscience Whigs, 109, 113
Conscription Act, 146
Constitution (New York), 28
Constitutional Union Party, 129
Cooper, James Fenimore, 18
Corwin, Thomas, 100, 105
Cotton Whigs, 109
Cox, Samuel Sullivan, 173
Cralle, Richard K., 61
Crawford, William H., 23
Crittenden, John J., 102, 134, 135
Cuba, 166
currency question, 165–66
Curtin, Andrew G., 177
Curtis, George William, 5, 57

Dana, Charles A., 56, 95, 134,
    137, 138
Darrow, Clarence, 50
Davis, David, 177
Davis, Henry Winter, 150
Davis, Jefferson, 152, 160
Davis, Noah, 172
Davis, Varina, 160
Day, Benjamin, 51
Delmar, Alexander, 175
Delmonico's, 144, 169
Democratic Party, 23, 25, 26, 43,
    86–89, 90, 97, 100, 106, 112,
    120, 121–22, 123, 125, 140,
    145, 172; and Dorr Rebellion,
    82; and draft riots, 145;
    nomination of Greeley, 155–56,
    157, 174, 178–79. *See also*
    Young America
*Democratic Review. See United
    States Magazine and Democratic
    Review*
Denver House Hotel, 126
Deposit-Distribution Act (1836),
    33

Devyr, Thomas, 77
Dial, 58
Dickens, Charles, 57
Distribution Bill, 34–35. *See also*
    land
Donnelly, Ignatius, 165
Dorr, Thomas, 80–81, 84
Dorr Rebellion, 66, 80–85, 127
Douglas, Stephen A., 95, 110,
    114–15, 125–26, 129, 138
Douglass, Frederick, 9, 99, 106,
    143, 150
draft riots (New York), 98, 132,
    143–49
Dred Scott decision, 124–25

East Poultney, Vermont, 10
Edgeworth, Maria, 62
Edwards, Justin, 15
elections: of 1836, 29–30; of
    1840, 21, 44–47; of 1848, 90–
    91, 99–107; of 1856, 123–24;
    of 1860, 128–29; of 1872,
    155–57, 174–80
emancipation, 140–43
Emancipation Proclamation,
    142–43
Emerson, Ralph Waldo, 58, 65,
    68, 73, 113
Emmet, Robert, 97
Equal Rights Party, 36. *See also*
    Locofocos
Erie Canal, 17
Erie *Gazette*, 11
Eugenie (empress of France), 169
Evans, George Henry, 74, 75, 77.
    *See also Radical; Working Man's
    Advocate*
Exeter Academy, 9

F. A. O. Schwarz, 169
Farmer's Cabinet, 13

Federalists, 10, 13, 22–23
Fenians, 166. *See also* Irish
    Americans
Fenton, Reuben E., 172, 176
Fessenden, William Pitt, 134
Field, David Dudley, 97
Fifteenth Amendment, 159, 174,
    176. *See also* Reconstruction
filibustering, 120
Fillmore, Millard, 109, 110–11,
    123
Fish, Hamilton, 116, 135
Fisk, Jim, 175
Fitzhugh, George, 49
Flourney, Thomas, 102
Folger, Charles, 172
Foner, Eric, 117, 118
Fourier, Charles, 66, 68, 77
Fourierism, 1, 66, 67–72. *See
    also* American Union of
    Associationists; Grand Prairie
    Harmonial Institute; North
    American Phalanx; Sylvania
    Phalanx
Fourteenth Amendment, 158, 174,
    176. *See also* Reconstruction
Fox, Katie, 66
Fox, Maggie, 66
Fredericksburg, Battle of, 139
Free Enquirer, 52
Free Soil Party, 106, 107, 111,
    113
Freedmen's Bureau Bill, 159. *See
    also* Reconstruction
Fremont, John C., 123–24, 150
French revolution of 1848, 94
Frisbee, Levi, 62
Fugitive Slave Law (1850), 113–14
Fuller, Margaret, 5, 50, 57–59, 95,
    99, 108. *See also Woman in the
    Nineteenth Century*

Garibaldi, Giuseppe, 94
Garnet, Henry Highland, 106
Garrison, William Lloyd, 38, 140,
    180
General Trades Union, 35, 82
George, Henry, 156
Georgia, 25, 180
German revolution of 1848, 94
Gettysburg, Battle of, 148
Giddings, Joshua, 89, 106
Godkin, E. L., 161
Godwin, Parke, 75, 150
Gould, Jay, 168, 175
Graham, Sylvester, 41, 66
Grand Prairie Harmonial Institute,
    70. *See also* Fourierism
Grant, Ulysses S., 149, 153, 157,
    173, 175, 177, 180
Granger, Francis, 111
Greeley, Arthur Young (Pickie),
    59, 108
Greeley, Gabrielle, 167
Greeley, Horace: *The American
    Conflict*, 149; on Anti-Rent
    War, 78–79; childhood, 7, 9;
    congressional career, 107–8;
    death of, 181; economic views,
    31–35; in election of 1848,
    101–7; on education, 9, 37–38;
    on emancipation, 140–43; and
    Federalists, 13; and Fourierism,
    67–72; on Irish American
    nationalism, 96–98; on labor, 36,
    171; and land reform, 73–75;
    Log Cabin Song Book, 46; on
    literature, 60–63; on nativism,
    122–23; *An Overland Journey*,
    126–27; personal life, 41–42,
    58–59, 108, 166–67; *Political
    Textbook for 1860*, 129; on
    property, 78–79; *Recollections*,

7, 12, 13; running for president, 155–57, 174–80; on secession crisis, 133–36; and temperance, 15, 65–66; *Why I Am a Whig*, 45; on women's rights, 99, 173, 174. *See also* Republican Party; slavery controversy; Whig Party
Greeley, Ida, 167
Greeley, Mary Youngs Cheney (Molly), 41–42, 58, 59, 108, 148, 155, 167, 174, 180
Greeley, Mary Woodburn, 8–9
Greeley, Raphael, 108
Greeley, Zaccheus (father), 8–9, 12, 166
Greeley, Zaccheus (grandfather), 8
Greeley Point, Wyoming, 181
"greenbacks." *See* currency question
Grinnell, Moses, 135
Gurowski, Adam, 95, 134

Hale, John P., 88
Hall, "Elegant Oakey," 172
Halstead, Murat, 175
Harlan, James, 104
Harper's Ferry, raid on, 127–28
Harris, Ira, 78
Harrison, William Henry, 21, 29–30, 45, 54, 85, 104
Hartford *Courant*, 82
Hawthorne, Nathaniel, 57, 62
Hay, John, 138, 139
Hedge, Frederick Henry, 58
Helper, Hinton Rowan, 129. *See also Impending Crisis of the South*
Herndon, William, 126
Hoar, Rockwood, 100
Hoe, Robert, 51
Hoffman, John T., 172

Holland Land Company, 77
Holt, Michael, 105
homestead bills, 107, 121, 165. *See also* land
Hone Club (New York), 18
Horace Greeley (ship), 181
Horace Greeley Memorial Highway, 181
Houston, Sam, 39
Howe, Daniel Walker, 61
"Hunkers," 89, 100, 105, 122
Hungarian revolution of 1848, 94
Hutcheson, Frances, 60

Impending Crisis of the South (1860), 129. *See also* Helper, Hinton Rowan
Independent, 167
Independent Treasury, 34
International Workingmen's Association, 170
Irish Americans, 95–98, 148–49, 169. *See also* repeal movement
Irish World, 97
Italy, 94

Jackson, Andrew, 4, 23, 27, 85; and Bank War, 25–26; and Indian removal, 24–25; and nullification, 25, 27
Jefferson, Thomas, 23
Jeffersonian, 1, 43–44
Jewett, William Cornell, 152
Johnson, Alvin, 180
Johnson, Andrew, 150, 158, 159; impeachment of, 161–62
Joint Committee on the Conduct of the War, 139

Kansas, slavery controversy in, 114–15, 119, 125

Kansas-Nebraska Act (1854), 113,
114
Keene, Laura, 153
Kendall, Amos, 25
Kennebunk *Journal*, 107
Kennedy, Grace, 63
Kent, James, 80
Kent Club (New York), 18
Knickerbocker, 61
Knights of St. Crispin, 170
Know-Nothing Party, 113, 122–23.
See also nativism
Kohl, Lawrence, 30

land, 34–35. *See also* Distribution
Bill; homestead bills
land reform, 66, 73–75. *See also*
Evans, George Henry; National
Reform Association
Leavitt, Joshua, 88
Lecompton Controversy, 125
Lee, Robert E., 149, 153
Leiber, Francis, 180
Liberal Republican Party, 1, 4,
157, 174–80
Liberator, 38
Liberty Party, 86–87, 88, 90, 106,
113
Livingston, Robert L., 77
Livingston Manor, 76
Lincoln, Abraham, 4, 22, 84,
93, 102, 107, 113, 125–26,
128–29, 131, 135–36, 137–39,
141–42, 149–53
Locke, John, 73
Locofocos, 36, 43. *See also*
Democratic Party; Equal Rights
Party
Log Cabin, 1, 45, 46
London Quarterly Review, 63

Lord, Samuel, 18
Lord and Taylor, 169
Louisville *Courier-Journal*, 175
Lovejoy, Elijah, 40
Luther, Seth, 81. *See also Address
on the Right of Free Suffrage*

Macy, Rowland, 169
Madison, James, 23, 26
Manassas. *See* Bull Run
Mangum, Willie P., 29
Mann, Horace, 8
Marble, Manton, 167
Marcy, William L., 44
Marshall, John, 38
Marx, Karl, 5, 50, 56, 95, 137
Mazzini, Guiseppe, 59, 94
McClellan, George, 139, 150
McDowell, Irvin, 138
McElrath, Thomas, 55, 86
McLean, John, 100, 105, 123
Memphis riot (1866), 163. *See also*
Reconstruction
Merchant's Exchange (New York),
17
Mercier, Henri, 151
Metropolitan Museum of Art,
169
Mexican War, 88–89, 101
Military Reconstruction Acts,
158
Mill, John Stuart, 4
Ming, Alexander, 36, 82
Missouri Compromise, 124, 134
Missouri *Democrat*, 175
Monroe, James, 26
Moore, Ely, 82
Morgan, William, 13
Morrill, Justin, 15
Morse, Samuel F. B., 18

Mott, Lucretia, 99
Murphy, Thomas, 176

Nast, Thomas, 179–80
National Intelligencer, 26
National Reform Association, 66.
   See also Evans, George Henry;
   land reform
National Republicans, 23, 26
nativism, 84, 87, 94, 111, 122–23.
   See also Know-Nothing Party
New England Emigrant Aid
   Company, 115
New Harmony, 65
New Orleans riot (1866), 163. *See
   also* Reconstruction
New Orleans *Tribune*, 177
New York (state), politics of 44,
   78, 82, 107, 171, 172
New York (city): rise of antebellum
   working class, 18; urban growth
   in 16–17, 167–69. *See also*
   draft riots
New York *Courier & Enquirer*, 69,
   88, 102
New-Yorker, 1, 41, 44, 60–63
New York *Evening Post*, 16, 18, 150
New York *Express*, 72
New York General Banking Law of
   1838, 33
New York *Herald*, 53–54, 138, 147
New York Philharmonic
   Orchestra, 169
New York Social Science Review,
   175
New York State Anti-Slavery
   Society, 38
New York *Sun*, 52, 54
New York Tribune, 1, 5, 47, 49–
   50, 51, 54–58, 60, 69, 88, 89–

90, 93, 95, 99, 101, 106, 115,
   133, 134, 137, 138, 147–48,
   161–62, 167, 174
Niagara Peace Conference (1864),
   152
Niles, Hezekiah, 28
Niles' Weekly Register, 11, 28
North American Phalanx, 71. *See
   also* Fourierism
North American Review, 60
Northern Spectator, 10–11
Norton, Andrews, 62

O'Brien, Smith, 97
O'Connell, Daniel, 96–97. *See also*
   repeal movement
Olmstead, Frederick Law, 115
Opdyke, George, 146
Ossili, Angelo, 59. *See also* Fuller,
   Margaret
Owen, Robert Dale, 52, 72, 82

Pacific railroad, 121
Paine, Thomas, 73
Paris Commune, 169
Parton, James, 46, 55, 69, 70, 95,
   107, 147, 148, 178, 180
Past and Present, 73. *See also*
   Carlyle, Thomas
Peabody, Elizabeth, 58
Pfizer, Charles, 144
Phillips, Wendell, 150, 160,
   164
Pierce, Franklin, 112, 114
Pike, James Shepard, 56, 134
Poe, Edgar Allen, 52
Polk, James K., 86, 87
Pomeroy, Samuel C., 150
popular sovereignty, 114, 125
Potter, David, 134

Poultney (Vermont), 8, 11
Preston, William B., 102
The Prostrate State (1873), 56

Radical, 74. *See also* Evans,
    George Henry
Raymond, Henry J., 44, 46, 56,
    69, 112, 117, 129
Reconstruction, 158–66
Redmond, Charles, 106
Regan, John H., 155
Reid, Whitelaw, 167, 177, 181
Rensselaerswyck, 76
repeal movement, 96. *See also*
    Irish Americans
Republican Party: origins, 1,
    113–17; ideology of, 118–21;
    in New York, 136–37; Radical
    Republicans, 139–40, 141,
    149–51, 159–60, 161, 171
Rhodes, James Ford, 49
Richardson, Albert D., 126
Rights of Man to Property! (1829),
    73. *See also* Skidmore, Thomas
Ripley, George, 57, 58
Rives, William Cabell, 134
Robinson, William E., 97
Rochester *Evening Post*, 72
Rust, Albert, 117

Saint-Simon, Claude Henri de,
    69
San Jacinto, Battle of, 39
Sanders, George N., 152
Schurz, Carl, 174
Scott, Winfield, 44, 100, 104, 111,
    112
secession crisis, 132–36
Sedgwick, Theodore, 97
Seneca Falls (New York), 93, 99

Seward, William Henry, 22, 29,
    43, 44, 78, 82, 88, 96, 100,
    105, 109, 110, 111, 117, 119,
    123, 128, 132, 136, 140, 151,
    166
Seymour, Horatio, 140, 145, 146,
    148
Shadrach, rescue of, 114
Sheridan, Philip, 161
Sherman, William T., 151
"Silver Gray Whigs," 111–12, 122
Simons, Thomas Y., 155
Sinclair, Samuel, 181
Skidmore, Thomas, 73. *See also*
    The Rights of Man to Property!
Slamm, Levi D., 82
slavery controversy, 3, 38–41,
    85–87, 93–129
Smith, Adam, 60
Smith, Gerrit, 38, 160
Smith, Joseph, 84
Social Destiny of Man (1840), 69.
    See also Brisbane, Albert
Society for the Diffusion of
    Political Knowledge, 145
South Carolina, 25, 132, 164
Southern Literary Messenger, 61
Specie Circular (1838), 33, 42
Spencer, Herbert, 175
Spirit of the Times (New York), 16
Springfield (Massachusetts)
    Republican, 125, 175
Squibb, Edward Robinson, 144
St. Nicholas Society (New York),
    18
Stanton, Edward M., 161
Stanton, Elizabeth Cady, 99, 174
Stanton, Henry, 99
Sterne, Simon, 175
Sterret, Joseph M., 11

Stephens, Alexander, 102
Stevens, Thaddeus, 8, 139, 164
Stone, E. G., 10
Strassburger, Albert, 155
Strong, George Templeton, 132, 151
Stuart, Alexander T., 169
Sumner, Charles, 89, 117, 132, 139
Sweeny, Peter, 172
Swisshelm, Jane, 99
Sylvania Phalanx, 70–71. See also Fourierism

Tallmadge, Nathaniel, 43
Taney, Roger B., 124
Tappan, Arthur, 8, 38
Tappan, Lewis, 8, 38
tariff, 12, 25, 87–88, 121, 165, 175, 178
Taylor, George Washington, 18
Taylor, Zachary, 100, 102, 104–5, 106, 109, 110, 111
Taxpayer's Union (New York), 168
Teesdale, John, 105
Texas: annexation of, 38, 85–86; independence of, 38, 85
Thayer, Eli, 115
Thirteenth Amendment, 141, 176
Thoreau, Henry David, 65, 156
Tiffany's, 169
Tilden, Samuel, 97
Tilton, Theodore, 150, 151
Tocqueville, Alexis de, 11
Toombs, Robert, 102
Tremaine, Lyman, 172
Tribune Association, 55
Trumbull, Lyman, 156, 177
Turner, Nat, 38
Twain, Mark, 5, 50, 127, 167, 179

Tweed, William Marcy, 167–68, 172
Tyler, John, 45, 81, 82, 85, 104, 134

Underwood, John C., 160
Union Club (New York), 18
Union League Club (New York), 161, 168
United States, history of: capitalist transformation, 3, 11–12, 144, 167–69; communications revolution, 50–54; Panic of 1819, 9; Panic of 1837, 34, 42–43, 60, 67; Second Great Awakening in, 14–15
United States Magazine and Democratic Review, 61. See also Democratic Review
Universalists, 15
Unitarianism, 60

Vallangdingham, Clement, 140, 151
Van Buren, John, 97
Van Buren, Martin, 21, 23, 28, 29–30, 34, 82, 86, 89, 100, 106
Vanderbilt, Cornelius, 160, 168, 180
Van Rensselaer, Stephen, 77
Villard, Henry, 126

Wade, Benjamin, 139
Walker, David, 38. See also Appeal to the Colored Citizens of the World
Walker Tariff, 87. See also tariff
Wallace, Mike, 169–70
Walsh, Mike, 81
Washington Peace Conference, 134–35

Watterson, Henry, 175
Webb, James Watson, 69, 88, 102, 112
Webster, Daniel, 25, 26, 29, 100, 104, 110, 111
Weed, Thurlow, 22, 28, 43, 44–45, 72, 88, 105, 109, 116, 117, 128, 129, 135, 136–37, 172
Wells, David Ames, 165
West, John T., 16
Westhaven (Vermont), 9
Whig Party, 1, 19, 24, 26–30, 44–47; and Anti-Rent War, 78–79; decline of, 109–12; on Dorr Rebellion, 82; economic views of, 30–35; moral views of, 37–38, 60; in New York, 28–29, 88, 111–12
White, Horace, 175
White, Hugh Lawson, 29
Whitman, Walt, 59, 168
Wilentz, Sean, 4, 80
Williams, Robert C., 9
Wilmot Proviso, 89–90, 100, 101, 102, 105, 110

Wilson, Henry, 125
Wirt, William, 14
Woman in the Nineteenth Century (1845), 58. *See also* Fuller, Margaret
women's rights, 99, 173–74. *See also* Seneca Falls
Wood, Fernando, 140, 145
Working Man's Advocate, 74. *See also* Evans, George Henry
Workingmen's Advocate, 52
workingmen's parties, 35–36, 73
Workingmen's Union, 171
Wright, Frances, 52, 72, 82
Wright, Silas, 89

Young, Brigham, 126
Young, John Russell, 161
Young America, 61, 152. *See also* Democratic Party
"Young Indians," 102
Young Ireland, 94, 97, 98

Zoar, 65

About the Author

Mitchell Snay was born in Chicago and educated at the University of Michigan and Brandeis University, where he received his PhD in the history of American civilization. He is the author of *Gospel of Disunion: Religion and Separatism in the Antebellum South* (1993) and *Fenians, Freedmen, and Southern Whites: Race and Nationality in the Era of Reconstruction* (2007), as well as the coeditor of *Religion and the Antebellum Debate over Slavery* (1998). Snay is currently the William T. Utter/Clyde E. Williams Professor of History at Denison University in Granville, Ohio, and lives with his wife and son in Columbus, Ohio.